The Threat of Tourism

Challenge to the Church

The Threat of Tourism

Challenge to the Church

Ron O'Grady

WCC Publications, Geneva

Cover design: Marie Arnaud Snakkers
Cover photo: René Arnaud

ISBN 2-8254-1481-6

150 route de Ferney, P.O.Box 2100
1211 Geneva 2, Switzerland
Website: http://www.wcc-coe.org

No. 113 in the Risk Book Series

Printed in Switzerland

This book is a recognition of
the Ecumenical Coalition on Tourism,
a relatively small network of Christians around
the world who have struggled for almost
25 years to make the church aware of those people
who have been the victims of tourism

Table of Contents

1. Behold the Tourist

> A man travels the world over in search of what he needs and returns home to find it.
>
> George Moore, 1852-1933

> I laugh when I hear that the fish in the water is thirsty,
> You wander restlessly from forest to forest
> While the Reality is within your own dwelling
> The truth is here!
> Go where you will to Benares or Mathura
> Until you have found God in your own soul
> The whole world will seem meaningless to you.
>
> Rabindranath Tagore, Bengali poet

By any measure, tourism is one of the most remarkable social developments in recent history. The figures are staggering. An industry which did not even exist 100 years ago has today become the world's largest commercial business with a current annual revenue estimated to be around 500 billion dollars or 11 percent of global gross domestic product. The World Tourism Organization (WTO) estimated there were 25 million international tourism arrivals in 1950. This number grew to 689 million in 2000 and is expected to reach 1.6 billion arrivals by 2020. An estimated 8 percent of the global work-force is engaged in the tourism industry (includes indirect/informal jobs) or 1 in every 12 workers.

Tourism is now such an internationally recognized phenomenon that every reader of this book can relate to it either from their own or their friends' experiences. Many will be frequent tourists for whom a regular holiday in distant lands has become a standard part of their life-style. Travel, they will tell you, has broadened the mind and given them fresh insights into the situation in other parts of the planet. And there is no question that for great numbers of people tourism has made a major contribution to their understanding of the world and at the same time provided them with genuine enjoyable experiences.

The positive aspects of tourism are promoted with regularity in the media. A constant stream of television travelogues, glossy magazines and newspaper articles provide information on interesting places to visit while saturation advertising has persuaded the general public that tourism is the ultimate positive, refreshing and exciting experience.

The cliches of tourism reinforce the illusion.

- Is your life boring? Let us take you on the adventure of a life-time.
- Are you overworked and stressed? We will give you a holiday in paradise on a sandy beach beneath wafting coconut palms.
- Are you curious about other people? Come to this island to savour the exotic way of life and enjoy new and strange traditions.
- Life is too ordinary for you? For a small price you can live like the rich and famous in a romantic hotel with servants to cater for your every whim.

Paradise – exotic – romantic! Small wonder tourism has become the panacea for all our problems. Tourism is constantly being dangled before us as an experience that provides meaning, happiness and the fulfilment of both our needs and our dreams. To new generations of busy people tourism has become their regular escape and highest pleasure.

Since some of the most popular (and cheapest) tourism destinations are those countries with a rather low economic standard of living, tourists will sometimes have a niggling concern about the effect of tourist hordes on the life and culture of the local people. But these fears are quickly put to rest by the conventional wisdom which claims that tourism is the best way for a country to develop its economy. It will seem obvious to visitors that tourism brings jobs to the locals and foreign currency for the country and this argument is a strong one in countries in desperate need of both these things. In addition, others will claim that the indigenous population in these countries is by nature hospitable to foreigners so they enjoy having the tourists come to their land. As so often happens in life, we interpret unknown situations in terms of our own needs and ambitions.

The sensitive tourist looking at tourism will certainly pick up clues to the underlying problems and will be aware of a few of the implications. But he or she will also be conscious of the way travel has the ability to expose people to the good, the true and the beautiful. These positive experiences of tourism are genuine and enduring. Tourism has indeed changed lives and attitudes for the better. In the beautiful words of Bengali poet Rabindranath Tagore,

> Thou hast made me known to friends whom I knew not,
> given me seats in homes not my own.
> Thou hast brought the distant near
> And made me a brother of the stranger.

Many travellers will echo these haunting sentiments and regale you with an account of the way an experience in a foreign culture helped to change their worldview.

While recognizing the pleasure and excitement of the genuine tourism experience we will, through most of this book, turn away from such accounts, valid though they are. In the wider picture we will try to hear the voices of people who have been exploited by the invasion of tourists. We will also begin to assess the effect this invasion has on the overall environment, on culture and on social and economic development. A few of the stories recounted will be located in the affluent part of the world but most occur in countries where there is extensive poverty or repression and where tourism can be exploited by the few at the expense of the many. In lands where they suffer from a repressive regime, the people's voice is obviously never expressed in tourism promotion, so it is our responsibility to listen to what is being said and make a reasonable response. Once we have heard these voices we will try to ask what ordinary people can do to stem a few of the injustices which will become evident as we go along.

Think of this book as a short journey through some of the tourism-related problems which contemporary society will have to face in the coming years. It may be your first introduction to what could one day become an increasingly serious problem for the whole of humankind.

2. Mass Tourism Takes Off

> Tourism, while being a potent force for good, has sadly turned into an activity that leaves in its trail massive numbers of victims.
>
> Samuel Kobia, general secretary,
> World Council of Churches, September 2005

February 9, 1969 was a brisk spring morning in the American town of Everett. The group of workers assembled at an airfield near the town knew that this day could mark a turning point in the history of travel but they were sufficiently realistic to realize that this day might instead mark one of the costliest misjudgments in industrial history.

All eyes were on the giant assembly plant beside the airfield – the world's largest ever building by volume with a space of 200 million cubic feet. Finally the doors opened and a huge plane rolled slowly out to be greeted by the watchers with gasps of astonishment followed by loud cheers.

The men and women watching were part of a team of 50,000 workers who had devoted the previous 16 months to the construction of a dynamic new aeroplane to be called the 747. They called themselves "the Incredibles" and they had undertaken to create aviation history by building the largest civilian aeroplane in the world.

The sight was breathtaking. The fuselage of the plane was 225 feet in length and the tail was as tall as a six-story building. To provide air pressurization the plane had to be filled with more than a ton of air. Built to accommodate up to 490 passengers and 33 crew, the cargo hold had to provide room for 3400 separate pieces of luggage. It had a cruising speed of 640 mph and a range of 6000 miles. Flying machines on this scale had never before been attempted. They called the new plane Jumbo.

The giant plane rumbled along the tarmac and finally lifted into the sky to the cheers of those on the ground. A new era in travel had just been opened and it was destined to change forever the way people would perceive the world.

Thirty plus years later we have become so accustomed to hundreds of these giant planes taking off from airports all around the globe that their size and significance fails to amaze. But if there was one significant date to mark the start of modern tourism it was that day in 1969 when the mass rapid transport of humans from any point on the earth to any other became possible.

In earlier years, tourism was confined to a slow movement from place to place by sea or land and the number of travellers was small and containable. As modern transport developed, the total number of tourists was still constrained by the relatively small size of ships and aircraft. The Jumbo jet brought an exponential change. International passenger numbers quickly escalated to the tens of thousands and soon to the tens of millions. The size of airports exploded. Today, large sporting events demonstrate how easy it has now become to move a million people to any one particular city in a matter of hours.

But even this growth is insignificant compared with what lies ahead. Tourism organizations continue to estimate even greater numbers of travellers in the future. Airbus and Boeing are both developing new planes which are more economical in their use of fuel and enable longer direct flights. Competition between the two aviation companies is fierce as they plan for the flying giants of the future. Airbus jumped to the front of the race in April 2005 when its new plane had a successful maiden flight. The Airbus A380 is designed to carry as many as 840 passengers between major airports and already has a large number of advance orders.

Giant planes plus mega cruise ships are part of our future and are warning us that what we now call mass tourism will very soon be moving from mass to massive.

3. The Impact of Tourism

> Tourism is like fire – out of control, it can burn down your house, but if you harness that energy, you can cook food with it…We want to make tourism a more positive force in the world.
>
> Costas Christ,
> Senior Director of Conservation International

> One person flying in an aeroplane for one hour is responsible for the same greenhouse gas emissions as a typical Bangladeshi in a whole year.
>
> Beatrice Schell,
> European Federation for Transport and Environment

If we had the time and money we could go to a hundred places on the earth's surface and record a whole series of isolated instances of the way certain kinds of tourism have left an ugly mark on a community.

- In the Himalayas, a group of young trekkers move along a well-worn trail among the great peaks. They stop at a camp site for the night and pitch their tents. Hunting around the area they uproot scraggy trees which provide the wood for a camp fire. Next day they move on, leaving all their waste – heaps of spent oxygen cylinders, broken glass, plastic bags, human waste and toilet paper which litter the region and could remain frozen in the ice for centuries. The Himalayas has been described as the world's highest junkyard.
- Western and Asian tourists walk up and down the streets of a small town near Phnom Penh in Cambodia. Inside the rows of houses, dim red lights reveal the features of young girls, some as young as seven years. The children have been abducted from their home villages by criminals and now are being kept as slaves to serve the child-sex tourists who fill the streets and bars. The tourists have learned about this

village from the internet and know they can bargain down the price of a girl to just a few dollars.

- In the lakeshore village in the Philippines 250 people are evicted by the police who move in and demolish their houses without warning. The local people have lived there for generations but a wealthy developer wants the land for an ecotourism development and has bribed the authorities to take it over. This kind of human-rights abuse is common in almost every third-world country where tourism development has taken place.
- From the autobahns of Germany going south to the highways of the United States leading to Yosemite, each year the tourist season marks the beginning of road congestion that will halt traffic for hours, pollute the atmosphere and lead to gridlock over miles of roading.
- Inside King Tut's little tomb in Egypt, the crush of tourists and the effect of their breath has increased the temperature to the point where a slimy fungus is discolouring the ancient wall paintings. The debate about the damage has been confusing. Politicians argue that they need the tourists but they also want to keep their heritage. The Egyptian government has since closed the tomb to all tourists. The Chinese government is facing the same problem with its warrior tomb in Xian.
- The Mexican resort of Cancun was developed 30 years ago when only 12 families lived on the island. Now it has 2.6 million visitors per year, the local mangroves have been rooted out and inland forests have been cut down. In the township, 75 percent of the sewage of the population is untreated.

Each one of these reported local stories is a small part of a much larger picture about the way tourism impacts on the daily life of people. Some of that impact can be positive for the local community, bringing employment and creative development. But other local communities have had the lives of all their people destroyed by the growth of an intrusive tourism. When that happens, the people become angry at the way tourism is affecting their land, their employment, the environment, the oceans, their religion or the life and customs. In the more extreme instances, their protest becomes personal and leads to local people stoning tourists or even firing rifle shots at a tourist bus. It is important that authorities understand this anger and attempt to remedy any injustice that has occurred.

In recent years many tourism industry leaders have appeared puzzled by the discovery that there are people who are negative about tourism. Seven years ago I addressed a gathering of around 600 tourism leaders at an international conference in the Philippines and spoke on the problem of child-sex tourism. The minister of tourism from a small tourism country bordering the Mediterranean immediately stood up to denounce the planners of the conference for letting this issue appear on the agenda. He argued that tourism is overwhelmingly positive, providing employment, enjoyment and foreign currency and it is essential for the growth of the tourism industry that we should never even discuss any of the negatives. Fortunately he was over-ruled and most of the following speakers took a more sympathetic approach to those children who are the victims of sex tourism. The attitude of the minister does, however, reflect the self-interest which has, until recently, characterized much tourism development around the world.

The tunnel vision which refused to see anything negative in tourism has changed to some degree. This change has occurred partly because the whole of the world's environment is undergoing severe degradation and this is now being recognized by governments and environmentalists alike. Scientists studying critical aspects of our world's environment have claimed that the global ecosystem is being endangered to the point where it poses a threat to human survival. While there are numerous reasons for this dangerous situation, tourism has to be recognized as a key contributor to at least some of the situations developing. In many places the role played by tourism is largely a consequence of the sheer weight of the number of people involved.

One of the increasingly quoted threats to survival is the growth of global warming. This has become a constant theme for scientists concerned about the health of the planet and each year yet more evidence is produced to indicate the dangers caused by the increase in greenhouse gases. It is now generally accepted that an excessive amount of carbon dioxide emissions has been a principal factor in this warming of the planet. One of the largest sources of CO_2 comes from transport and especially from the aeroplane. Tourism is therefore seen as a major contributor to environmental degradation.

Tourism numbers escalate each year and tourists become more mobile, travelling greater distances and exploring ever more remote regions. Tourist passengers already account for more than 60 percent of all international travellers and therefore contribute a major share of the growth in greenhouse emissions. One study estimated that a single transatlantic return flight emits almost half the CO_2 emissions produced by all other sources (lighting, heating, car use, etc.) consumed by an average person yearly.[1] Airlines have recognized this fact and are themselves becoming concerned. British

Airways now has an official policy to reduce carbon dioxide emissions and has announced its success in making a significant reduction in its overall aircraft emissions in the past five years.

In addition to greenhouse gases from planes, tourism also produces other pollutants. The atmosphere is a clear indicator of environmental problems and tourism's contribution to local air pollution is graphically evident in many tourist centres. Returning to Northern Thailand in early 2005, several years after my previous visit, I was saddened to see that the beautiful mountain-top Doi Suthep Temple is no longer visible from the town of Chiangmai because of fog and pollution in the air. Looking back from the temple itself, the city below sits beneath a haze of pollutants. Some of the causes of this air pollution are specific to tourist activities. At all the tourism stops, tour buses leave their motors running for hours, pumping clouds of smog into the air while the tourists go for an excursion after which they return to a comfortably air-conditioned bus. In cold climates they will expect to return to a heated bus.

The worldwide effect of climate change is hard for us to comprehend and will, by its nature, require serious action on the part of governments and intergovernmental organizations; but in the following chapters we will note smaller, local situations where tourism is a threat to a specific environment and where informed local action has sometimes produced significant change.

Where tourism begins to expand its influence into a new local area, it is especially important that the people who live there be consulted and become participants in the planning of new or alternative tourism developments. Some care at this point could save problems later. We need to learn from past mistakes and have proper environmental impact studies carried out before damage is done.

In many places it is already too late. Irreparable damage has been done. This is particularly evident at tourism destinations in coastal areas. Resorts at the beach have always been immensely popular with tourism developers but the construction of facilities frequently takes place with little respect for the foreshore environment. The draining and filling of wetlands, the removal of mangrove swamps and the destruction of coral reefs help to erode the local ecosystem and can often cause long-term or permanent damage. When marinas and breakwaters are added, they change the currents and the coast line. In such fragile areas tourism is a major contributor to the damage incurred but with more sensitivity it could play a different role by protecting vulnerable ecosystems.

Well-researched evidence about the negative effects of tourism has been available for some years and it has became self-evident that if tourism continues to grow at its present pace it could be in danger of destroying the very things that are its attraction. A beautiful beach in a fragile environment is, for example, easily destroyed by too many people or by indiscriminate development.

A mounting number of examples of irresponsible tourism development led tourism agencies to begin the quest for a new approach to tourism. At the international level a number of intergovernmental organizations began to argue that strong measures would be necessary if tourism is to remain sustainable. The United Nations Environmental Programme (UNEP) reflected a growing hard line when it issued a declaration in 1997 stating, "Tourism should be restricted and, where necessary, prevented, in ecologically and culturally sensitive areas."[2]

The United Nations was made aware of the serious nature of the situation and, despite some reservations, agreed to accept a leadership role in formulating a more responsible form of tourism. Following consultation with tourism leaders the United Nations proclaimed the year 2002 as the International Year of Ecotourism (IYE). In the curious language of intergovernmental agencies, the UN described the year thus:

> The International Year of Ecotourism will offer an opportunity to review ecotourism experiences worldwide, in order to consolidate tools and institutional frameworks that ensure its sustainable development in the future. This means maximizing the economic, environmental and social benefits from ecotourism, while avoiding its past shortcomings and negative impacts.[3]

As could be expected from such an introduction, the IYE spawned hundreds of conferences, consultations and seminars and issued thousands of reports, papers and books on the subject of ecotourism. At the end of this talkfest at least three fairly predictable facts seem to have been established.

- Primarily the IYE showed beyond doubt that some tourism activities are having a serious negative impact on various parts of the earth's ecosystem and this negative impact appears to be increasing.
- While there is genuine concern about this development, the monitoring and policing of negative practices which affect the environment is extremely difficult to maintain when tourism is given such a major role in a nation's economic development.

- Because of IYE, tourism developers began to develop large numbers of new "ecotourism" projects around the world.

The last fact has already caused problems. During the IYE, businesses created camps and eco-lodges, and natural resource managers were kept busy designing trails and tours. It was as if the label "ecotourism" on any tourism activity would automatically ensure that it was clean, green and acceptable. But the branding exercise took place without universally accepted guidelines or enforceable practices and almost every new tourism project indiscriminately had the label "ecotourism" attached to its advertising and publicity.

Despite all the warnings not to make IYE a "sales year" for ecotourism, one of the stated objectives of the Year was to "increase opportunities for the efficient marketing and promotion of ecotourism destinations and products on international markets".[4] In this at least the IYE was successful.

The NGO community had warned against these potential problems when looking forward to the IYE. Speaking to the UN Commission on Sustainable Development in 1999 an NGO report summarized the problem:

> Tourism is not, as people assert, a clean and non-polluting industry. A major problem is the lack of a common understanding of what sustainable tourism or ecotourism means. This ambiguity leads to violations of environmental regulations and standards. Hence, the environmental problems evolving from tourism are manifold. First of all, the tourism industry is very resource- and land-intensive. Consequently, the interest of the tourism sector will often be in conflict with local resource and land use practices. The introduction of tourism will imply an increased stress on resources available. An influx of tourists into the area

> will lead to a competition for resources. Employees working at the tourist sites compound this competition. Almost as a rule, tourists are supplied at the expense of the local population.[5]

The aims of IYE are clearly worthy ones even if their implementation is lacking. In simple terms, ecotourism is a call for tourism to be of such a nature

- that it has a minimal impact on the environment;
- that it respects local culture; and
- that it respects the dignity and the rights of local people.

Add to these IYE aims the obvious economic requirement which means that tourism must pay its way and distribute its profits fairly and we can formulate a positive summary of the goals of an acceptable form of tourism:

- ecologically responsible;
- socially acceptable;
- economically just and viable.

But as the record shows, all three of these are vulnerable. Despite a few successful ventures these overall goals are still far from being achieved.

4. A Tourism Which Is Is Ecologically Responsible

> Only by safeguarding the quality and viability of the environment and local communities will the tourism product be able to flourish.
>
> Ed Fuller, President of Marriott International 2004

> Treat the earth well -
> It was not given to us by our parents
> But loaned to us by our children.
>
> Kenyan proverb

There are some natural disasters which cannot be anticipated or prevented and we just have to live with the way these so-called "acts of God" threaten the environment. But most of the current threats to human survival are coming from our own actions – often as the consequence of human ignorance or greed. As the number of humans on the planet increases, the pressure on our whole ecosystem continues to grow. Conservationists identify ways in which our modern life-style is damaging the environment but it seems probable that our future survival is going to depend to a large degree on changing habitual life-styles so that we walk more softly on the earth. This is beginning to be understood in many areas as governments move to protect those parts of our planet that are vulnerable and try to curb aspects of consumption and activity which pose particular threats.

In this race to protect the world for future generations we have to look at every aspect of human activity, and tourism is certainly one of the key areas of human behaviour which is under the spotlight.

Uncontrolled conventional tourism must be considered as a contributor to the overall degradation of the environment around the world. The arrival of thousands (millions) of people at the same desirable tourism centre exerts enormous pressure on the natural environment and contributes towards such things as soil erosion, increased pollution, discharge of effluent into the ocean, the loss of natural wildlife habitats and the threat to endangered species of plant and animal life. Tourism puts added strain on limited basic resources such as water and food supplies and can place local populations in a situation where their own basic needs become secondary to the demands of the tourists.

Fortunately, all these threats could be countered if there is forethought and care. Tourism is, in fact, a unique activity insofar as it can both contribute to the threats to the environment but, if done properly, can also be a vehicle for protecting the environment. This latter hope was clearly the unrealized goal of those who worked to make tourism more sustainable in the International Year of Ecotourism. The IYE forced countries to identify more precisely those areas where the ecosystems of the planet are in danger and to begin to assess these situations in relation to tourism.

The record is not good.

Coral reefs

> Our oceans are under serious stress from pollution and trash, destructive fishing practices and uncontrollable tourism. We all share this responsibility, and we have to start believing that each and every one of us can make a difference.
>
> Susan Sarandon, Hollywood actress and eco-activist

Among the most fragile parts of the ocean, coral reefs face the threat of almost total destruction. Marine scientists believe that 10 percent of the world's coral reefs have been destroyed already and a further 70 percent could be dead by the year 2050 unless there is a change in our treatment of them. At a UN conference on climate change, experts from 98 countries concluded that less than 5 percent of the world's reefs are in a healthy state. Pollution, overfishing, rising temperatures, coastal development and diseases are among major threats to reefs.[6]

Although not the main contributor to the destruction of coral reefs, tourism was cited as one of the human activities which had helped create the problem. The stunning beauty of the reefs draws tourists in their millions and, in several islands and small countries, reef-related tourism has become a major feature of tourism promotion. But as with so many things in tourism, the very thing which attracts the tourists is in danger of being partially destroyed by the tourists themselves. Popular tourist bays in the Caribbean which used to have extensive coral reefs 30 years ago today report that the reefs have virtually disappeared.

Beach tourism resorts are often established in remote areas where there is minimal infrastructure. In such places, raw sewage is simply pumped into the sea in water near reefs. Even when septic tanks are installed, waste will often leak into the waters. Not only does this pollute the sea water but the sewage has nitrogen that affects marine plants and promotes the growth of algae, which blocks the path of sunlight to the reef and leads to its decay.

Tourists are usually insistent on getting as close to the reefs as possible. Boating, scuba diving, snorkelling and catching tropical fish for sale to tourists can have a negative effect on the reef. Small tour boats anchoring on or near reefs cause damage. Tourists walking on or near reefs stir up sediment and contribute to reef destruction from loss of sunlight. The more insensitive tourists will break off a piece of coral to take home as a souvenir of their visit.

Cruise ships are a direct threat to coral reefs by damaging them with their anchors or even accidentally hitting the reef with the ship's hull. A single cruise ship's anchor and chain will weigh as much as five tons and can damage an area of the ocean floor half the size of a large football field. To protect reefs, some cruise lines are now planning the itinerary of their ship so that wastewater is held aboard the ship while in this area. The wastewater is then released several nautical miles seaward of the reef.

In a few resorts, tourism operators are attempting to reduce the damage to reefs through tourist awareness campaigns and by establishing marine parks. One major success of the past five years has been the introduction by the Australian government of strict guidelines to protect one third of the Great Barrier Reef. The United States is considering the introduction of similar prohibitions off the coast of Hawaii and Florida.

Much more could be done to protect the world's reefs. The best measure would be to impose restrictions of access to the reefs themselves but there are few local politicians or tourism operators who would be willing to agree to this step. When the authorities weigh up the present value of the reefs to tourism against the long-term needs of the reef it is usually immediate profit which wins the contest. This failure to act by authorities means that long-term prospects for the rejuvenation of the reefs are bleak. At one time large cities such as Hong Kong, Singapore, Manila and Honolulu all had thriving coral reefs. As a result of human intervention, many of these reefs have long since disappeared. How long can our remaining reefs survive against the invasion?

The mountain trek

> Of all the "isms" of the 20th century, we may find that "tourism" is the worst.
>
> Prince Sadruddin Aga Khan

Mountains have always held a fascination for humankind. More recently, the soaring peaks have been seen as a place of escape from the stress of modern society and it is estimated that today more than 50 million tourists visit the mountains each year. Tourism is both an opportunity and a threat for mountain regions. While tourism revenues are now a major source of income for mountain communities, the growing number of visitors is a danger to their unique environment. The problem is exacerbated by the fact that mountain tourism often takes place in remote areas and is one of the least regulated sectors of world tourism.

Tourism in the high mountains poses distinctive environmental questions because of the alpine climate and ecology. It is a rule for those who hike the mountain trails that all non-biodegradable garbage must be carried out by trekkers. A short walk along any Himalayan trail will indicate that this rule is often ignored. Plastic water bottles float in remote mountain streams; cast-off batteries thrown on the ground create a serious form of toxic pollution throughout the hills; some trekkers seem unwilling to dispose of their own human waste in an appropriate manner; others wash themselves with soap or shampoo in lakes, streams or hot springs to add to the pollution of the waters while small mountains of waste products left by earlier trekkers line the tracks in festering piles. In the early 1990s, a clean-up campaign supported by young environmentalists took away 33 tons of rubbish and waste from the Mount Everest base camp area alone. The trail of waste left behind in the more popular tracks has led to them being described by guides as "Coca-Cola trail" and "toilet paper trail". This same irresponsible behaviour occurs in developed countries as well. Climbers on America's Mount McKinley have left human waste that is so insanitary and virus laden that in 2002 more that a quarter of all climbers reported having trouble with diarrhoea.[7]

For people living in the mountains, tourism creates problems for survival. Since very few shrubs or small trees are able to grow above the snow line, wood is a valuable commodity and essential for the wellbeing of mountain dwellers. Trekkers need camp fires for cooking and for warmth and are often careless with their indiscriminate use of the small trees they find. It has been estimated that one trekking tourist in Nepal – an area already suffering the effects of deforestation – can use four to five kilograms of wood a day.

In mountain areas, sport-based tourism is booming. It has expanded from the traditional areas of North America, the Nordic countries and the European Alps to new and largely untouched mountain regions in Central Asia, the Himalayas, the Andes and even Antarctica. Traditional mountain activities such as hiking, skiing, snowboarding and climbing have led to extreme sports such as bungee jumping, hydrospeeding, paragliding and canyoning.

The quote from Prince Sadruddin Aga Khan which heads this section is an expression of his frustration at the way sport tourism is destroying parts of the European Alps. His charity *Alp Action* claims that some parts of the Alps have become an ecological catastrophe, particularly the Haute Savoie region of the French Alps, which he blames on a French political decision to develop mass tourism. "The Alps", he claims, "are the water tower of Europe and, through the glaciers, its largest air-conditioning machine."[8]

Mountain snow-fields are in increasing demand with new and larger developments dotting mountain landscapes. The need for restrictions on their development is evident. Building ski runs often involves destroying swathes of forest, planting pylons for chairlifts and cable cars and building roads and tunnels. In the Alps, emission from millions of vehicles bringing visitors to the slopes threatens the health of trees and worsens the effects of global warming. Paths and ski runs harm sensitive mountain ecosystems and disturb plant and animal life.[9]

For mountain people in poorer regions of the world, there is ambivalence about tourism because there are benefits as a result of tourism revenues. In places where living standards have improved, young men and women now have the option of building a future in their home community instead of joining the exodus to the cities. Mountain people also have a market for their local crafts.

Tourism need not be a destructive force. It can provide benefits for mountain people if sensitively planned and managed. For this to happen, the development and control of tourism in mountain areas must be done in consultation with the local people and they must have the right to receive a fair proportion of the profits.

From pole to pole

> Tourist operators are beginning to tap into the huge demand to visit the last great wilderness on earth. Paradoxically both science and tourism have the

potential to damage the very qualities that draw them to Antarctica.

Australian Antarctic Division

From the highest points in the planet to the bottom of the world, no place of beauty escapes the eagle eye of the tourism developer. For those who have seen everything, the Antarctic polar cap has long been a desirable place to visit. Recognizing the fragility of the great white continent, tourism was actively discouraged by the nation-states which have bases in Antarctica.

Eventually these countries gave in to pressure and permitted limited tourism with certain restrictions on its activity. In 1991, tour operators set up their own self-regulatory body known as the International Association of Antarctic Tour Operators (IAATO). At that stage the annual number of tourists to Antarctica was around 5000 but by 2003 the numbers had exceeded 22,000.

In June 2003 the Antarctic Treaty nations met in Madrid and agreed that the region must be protected and that meant that tourism should be curbed. While recognizing that tourism operators had done their best to regulate the flow of tourists, a more stringent and possibly independent regulatory body was needed.

The need for such a body is evident. New operators are eyeing the Antarctic as a destination for tourism and plan to send cruise ships carrying up to a thousand passengers to the region. Many of these shipping companies are not members of IAATO and the potential for disaster is obvious since few of the new ships planning to sail south in 2006 have strengthened hulls to protect them against icebergs and pack ice. The possibility of an accident causing a leak from large vessels loaded with bunker oil is worrying. It could create a major catastrophe in a region which is still largely pristine.

Of even greater concern to the Treaty nations is the proposal for so-called "adventure tourism" being promoted by tourism entrepreneurs. The proposal to let tourists embark on ambitious and often highly dangerous expeditions in Antarctica is viewed with considerable anxiety by the Treaty nations, not only for the danger it poses to the tourists but also the complications which can arise if nearby countries have to send rescue teams to the region, risking their own lives in trying to save foolhardy tourists.

Heritage sites

> With all these tourists around you would think they would put in an elevator.
>
> Unknown tourist overheard at a Greek heritage site.

> What the people of Machu Picchu want is for tourism to be sensitive to their culture, religion, traditions and people.
>
> David Ugarte, former mayor of Cusco

Machu Picchu is South America's best-known archaeological site. Set high in the peaks of the Andes, it is believed to have been the main sanctuary city of the ancient Inca empire. The empire collapsed in just five years at the hands of Spanish *conquistadores* but Machu Picchu was never conquered and lay hidden in the jungle for centuries until it was rediscovered by the American explorer Hiram Bingham in 1911.

Today Machu Picchu is struggling to cope with its fame and the consequent crowds of tourists visiting it every year. The numbers continue to increase. In 2004 an estimated half a million tourists made their way to the citadel. Tourists arrive at Machu Picchu Pueblo which is the starting point for the climb along the old Inca trail. A noisy little town whose population has grown from 500 to 4000 in less than a decade, it is a reflection of the chaotic way tourism has developed around the Machu Picchu site. Hygiene is minimal with untreated human waste pumped into the nearby river.

The situation around the area became so serious that in January 2004 UNESCO threatened to place Machu Picchu on its list of endangered sites unless the Peru government got its act together and made major changes to the management of this world heritage site. Placement on this list could impose legal requirements that would limit access to the citadel.

One of the major problems is the unrestricted numbers and the inadequacy of the controls on their activity. Every day an average of 1500 tourists follow the 500 year old Inca trail for its full length of 40 miles, passing spectacular granite terraces and climbing up steps of stone. Some independent studies of the site have recommended that the number of trekkers on the track should be reduced to no more than 300 persons a day if the track is to survive.

In the Machu Picchu citadel itself there are up to 2000 visitors daily and this number is increasing by at least 6 percent every year. UNESCO says that number of tourists should be cut to 800 and adds that they should wear soft shoes to reduce pressure on the ruins. The Peruvian National Institute of Culture which is in charge of the day-to-day running of Machu Picchu has dismissed the UNESCO figure and claims the site could receive more visitors than at present. The administrator of the site has gone on record as saying that Machu Picchu could cope with 3000 tourists every day.

Behind the scenes a transnational enterprise, the *Orient Express*, has a monopoly on much of the tourism movement into the area. The company owns the airline which flies to the area and also the main luxury hotel. It was behind the plan to construct a cable car to transport tourists up to the entrance of Machu Picchu. The project would have involved considerable earth works and land removal and not surprisingly sparked off worldwide opposition. Fortunately the proposal has been defeated but it is still not forgotten and the private investors continue to press for its construction.

There is, of course, a vested interest in the authorities keeping the numbers high because of the money that the tourists bring into the country. A charge of US$20 per head has been imposed for an entrance ticket to the site. The result of this contribution is that Machu Picchu generates $6 million a year for the government, while the Inca trail brings in a further US$3 million. Local people keep hoping this money will help to bring improvement in the maintenance of the site and the neighbouring town but there is little evidence of this so far.

The threat of UN sanctions has forced the Peruvian government to act quickly and the experts drew up a proposal to preserve the Machu Picchu site from the ravages of tourism, thus avoiding the loss of its status as a world heritage site. They submitted a $132.5 million plan to the United Nations' cultural body in April 2005 and at present the proposal is still under consideration As a provisional concession the authorities have limited the number of daily visitors to 2500 from January 2006.

There are now almost 800 heritage sites around the world and most of them have, like Machu Picchu, become the focus of a tourism influx. They include such well known sites as the Great Wall of China, the Acropolis in Greece, Borobudur in Indonesia, Stonehenge in England and Angkor Wat in Cambodia. All face similar problems. As reminders of a former age, they no longer have any commercial value apart from being a tourist destination. But as their popularity grows so the number of tourists increases, with long queues waiting to visit the site. The added numbers, together with increased commercial activity around the site, place a great strain on the infrastructure, the region and the site itself.

Wildlife

> Man is the cause of all the destruction. If left unchecked, our actions will place plants, animals and humans at risk.
>
> Dr David Suzuki, November 1999

Much of the world's wildlife has been threatened with extinction through the inroads of civilization and many species of animal and bird are now on the endangered list. Among the contributors to this decline are decades of overhunting, poaching animals to sell ivory, farming and the inroads which human development makes on the natural habitat of creatures. Tourism is an ambivalent activity which has the potential to protect wild-life but when it is done incompetently it also becomes part of the threat to wildlife.

The downside of tourism is most obvious when it intrudes on the natural behaviour of the animals. Nature tourism is dependent on biodiversity being maintained and needs to preserve unique and abundant environments to attract the tourist. When the land and the natural resources are pressured by large numbers of visitors and excessive development, this biodiversity is easily lost. The impact on wildlife, vegetation, the foreshore and mountain life can be changed to the point where the animal-carrying capacity is reduced and sometimes lost altogether.

Animals can change their behavioural patterns under the pressure of tourism. Cross-country safaris invade the natural habitat of animals, causing stress and adaptation. Some tourism operators make a practice of chasing the animals in vehicles or light aircraft. The noise and intrusion into the daily life of animals affects their development. In cases recorded in Kenya, it has led to animals becoming so disturbed that they have neglected their young or failed to mate.

The other side of the coin is that if tourism is well managed, it can have a positive effect on wildlife preservation and protection and help to protect endangered species.

Consider the gentle turtle. Found in many parts of the planet, it is prized for the delicacy of its meat and upmarket restaurants have always served turtle soup as a specialty dish. The eggs of the turtle are also in demand and are swallowed whole with alcohol in popular bars from Asia to the Caribbean. Although most countries now prohibit the killing of turtle, poachers continue to capture them for sale to restaurants and steal the eggs for sale to tourists and villagers.

But in more recent years, tourists around the world have discovered the attraction of watching giant turtles lay their eggs in the sand and subsequently seeing the young turtles scamper to the ocean. So long as it is properly controlled, it is possible that this new attention on the turtles will be their salvation. From loggerhead turtles in Greece to green turtles in Costa Rica, environmentalists are setting new guidelines for protecting the turtles and securing government support for their efforts. Local people are discovering that they can make more money from the tourists than they can from stealing the eggs. The turtles are still not out of danger but if authorities move faster in providing protection they may yet survive.

The great apes and pandas are two other species being used to attract ecotourists. Non-governmental organizations in Africa and Asia have been working on methods of isolation which will permit a kind of limited tourism viewing for such creatures but not so close as to endanger the animals from infection or unwanted attention. If the methods are appropriate, the use of the animals for promoting tourism will hopefully prevent the poaching and unwanted killing which would otherwise be their fate.

Where animals and other wildlife need protection, responsible governments have established wildlife reserves and bird sanctuaries in which species can be protected against poachers and the inroads of property development. If well managed, native sanctuaries can be financed by revenues from nature-loving tourists. The effectiveness of this programme is shown when endangered species have begun to increase in numbers.

In Tanzania, strict anti-poaching laws in reserves are at last starting to take effect and the numbers of big game have shown a significant increase. The elephant population suffered badly from poaching in the 1970s and 1980s and fell to around 55,000 in 1989. A report from the tourism minister of Tanzania, April 2005, said the present number of elephants has increased to 120,000. Similar increases have been recorded for the number of lions appearing in the Serengeti. Tourist numbers increase when wildlife is protected.

Less visible than animals, smaller species of wildlife and native plants face similar threats to their survival. Hawaii is currently playing host to more than seven million tourists a year, six times the local population.

While this has helped the booming economy and provided a low unemployment rate it has brought unexpected damage to the environment. Recently, *The Economist* reported a rising tide of protest from environmental groups in Hawaii concerned at the loss of the unique birds, snails and plants found in the islands.[10] It reported that the US Fish and Wildlife Service currently lists 317 species, including 273 plants, in the Hawaiian Islands which are threatened or endangered – the highest number of any state in the nation. Environmental groups and local residents blame the pollution of cruise ships and the invasion of tourist numbers for this damage.

Cruise ships

People in the cruise-ship industry think big. In 1999, ship builders in Finland constructed the giant mega-ship *Voyager* in record time using a revolutionary module building method. When launched it was hailed as the largest passenger ship ever built. Within a few years the rival Cunard line spent $800 million to construct an even larger ship, the Queen Mary 2, the biggest (151,400 tons), longest, tallest and widest passenger liner ever built. In its first full year of operation it carried almost 130,000 passengers.

Shipyards cannot keep up with the demand for new cruise ships. At least 20 new mega-ships are scheduled to be built over the next two years (2005-2007). Some of those already in production will reach up 18 decks high into the sky and have accommodation for 3600 passengers and 1400 crew.

With so many new mega-ships entering the cruise market, the number of passengers is escalating at a much faster rate than most other forms of tourism. The cruise sector of tourism already transports around ten million passengers every year and is expected to grow by a remarkable 8.5 percent per year over the next decade.

Despite its popularity, or perhaps because of it, the cruise industry attracts considerable negative publicity from environmentalists. The discharge of marine pollution through oily bilge water and garbage is a regular practice in a number of ships but the size of the fleets makes the monitoring of bad practice difficult and it is costly to produce substantive evidence. However, several marine disasters have made authorities more vigilant. On the Western seaboard of America and in the Caribbean, the monitoring of cruise ships has become more proactive, with the result that several shipping companies have been convicted for illegal discharge of wastewater or for air pollution. The Royal Caribbean Cruises Ltd (which promotes itself as "environmentally friendly") paid $18 million in fines after pleading guilty to 21 counts of polluting the waters, lying to the court and illegally storing hazardous waste. Cruise ships try to save costs by dumping large amounts of hazardous chemicals at sea. They produce a range of waste chemicals from such things as dry cleaning and printing photographs. Some ships have secret bypass pipes to dump oil and hazardous materials overboard at night.[11]

While cruise ships are only a small percentage of the world's shipping fleet, the size of their crew and passenger list means they produce a mountain of waste. An added problem is that they generally follow similar routes and make regular visits to the same ports. Most of these cruise routes are in the more vulnerable and eco-sensitive regions of the world – areas where ocean pollution is already at its most serious. These include the Caribbean, the Mediterranean, Western Mexico, the Panama Canal Zone and the South Pacific.

The most popular route for cruise ships has been the wider Caribbean, stretching from Florida to French Guiana and including all the small islands which have made tourism their prime industry. This region receives around 63,000 port calls from cruise ships each year, generating at least 82,000 tons of garbage. The average ship carries 600 crew members and 1400 passengers and, on average, passengers on the Caribbean cruise ship are estimated to account for 3.5 kilograms of garbage per person per day.[12] Solid waste from passengers includes glass, paper, cardboard, aluminium and steel cans, incinerator ash, plastics and kitchen grease. Much of this non-hazardous waste is not easily biodegradable and some will end up on the ocean bed. The Hellenic Marine Environment Protection Association has studied the degradation of this waste and estimates that the time taken for objects to biodegrade in the ocean ranges from cotton cloth which takes 1-5 months, to tin cans 100 years, aluminium cans 200-500 years and a plastic bottle 450 years. The waste continues to accumulate on the beaches and ocean bed as a threat to marine life and a pollutant to the purity of the waters.

Most leading cruise lines have been challenged by the growing emphasis on ecotourism to implement practices and procedures that will reduce the amount of pollution they generate. It is, of course, in their own interests that they should do this. Clean oceans are essential if the cruise experience is to be appreciated and passengers do not want to disembark at contaminated beaches. By its nature, cruise-ship tourism needs a healthy, clean and natural environment.

A sustainable environment

> We are descending into an ecological debt we may not be able to repay.
>
> Prof. Ian Spellberg

The issue of sustainability is much wider than the continuance of tourism. It is a debate which is certain to occupy the best scientific minds in the coming decade. In March 2005, the Millennium Ecosystem Assessment was released. Based on the extensive and painstaking work of 1300 scientists in 95 countries it delivered a stark warning about the future of planet Earth. The scientists were agreed that we can no longer take the earth's resources for granted. The air, water and soil which sustain human life on earth are all under threat. The report gives irrefutable evidence that unless human behaviour is drastically modified, mass degradation of the environment will bring ecological dead zones and possibly lead to the collapse of life on earth.

Tourism is only one of the human activities which threaten the environment, but because of its size and growth it plays a significant role in the overall decimation of the planet. All the evidence in the preceding pages points to the wasteful use of earth's resources to meet the wishes of an industry which is essentially based on human enjoyment rather than human need. This is not to discount the importance of enjoyment but if that enjoyment comes at the expense of other people or poses a threat to the environment and possibly even to our own survival then it will have to come under serious scrutiny.

Leaders in the tourism industry have begun to explore ways to enforce what they call sustainable tourism. The United Nations Environmental Programme has listed this as one of its priorities and is attempting to promote the idea among government agencies and the tourism industry. They are looking for far more stringent laws for the management of sensitive areas and want governments to implement multilateral environmental agreements related to tourism.[13] If the scientists are right, it will take more than United Nations' resolutions to protect the earth but at least it is a starting point in helping us take specific action.

Given the huge economic importance of tourism to countries it is most unlikely there will be any voluntary reduction in tourism growth or development. But do we have the physical resources to sustain the kind of growth in tourism numbers which is now being contemplated and if so will it be at the expense of our own quality of life? If this cannot be done the possibility of more stringent laws and prohibitions might be the only recourse for the international community.

Already our universal access to such essential natural resources as oil and clean water cannot be guaranteed very far into the future and demand for resources could eventually exceed supply. The shortages will be exacerbated by a mobile population of millions of tourists moving around the planet every day of the year. No matter how sensitive their activity it can only accentuate the pressures on the environment and make a final solution so much more difficult.

At a purely selfish level, the tourism industry itself must find a sustainable form of tourism which does not waste natural resources nor harm the environment of places being visited. If it fails in this there is the real danger of imploding into self-destruction.

5. A Tourism Which Is Socially Acceptable

Tourism is now such a normal part of everyday life that its implications are seldom considered. Crossing borders has become such a commonplace event for people that it has lost its magic and challenge so that the distinction between national and international travel is seldom considered. However, this does not change the basic reality that travel to a foreign country is not a neutral action. Each time tourists pass through the immigration counter of a foreign territory they need to recognize that entry into this land is a privilege, not an automatic right. By entering as a tourist, visitors are automatically guests in a new and sometimes alien environment. As guests, tourists should act with sensitivity to cultural, ethnic, social, economic and religious ways of life which are different from those of their homeland. The differences reflect values which the tourist may or may not understand and which may or may not be acceptable in the tourist's homeland. Even so, visitors must recognize the values of their hosts and act in a manner which shows respect.

Respecting the local culture takes place when there is a genuine human encounter. The interactions between the host and the visitor are the life-changing experiences with give travel its unique charm. Friendships develop in the relationships of travel. In Asia, the age-old practice of bargaining was originally a way of establishing a relationship before the exchange of money and goods took place. Travellers today sometime approach bargaining in the market as if it is a confrontation or argument but when seen as building a relationship it can become an understandable and positive experience. Travel is an opportunity to break out of familiar patterns and gain insights into the cultures that make up the diversity and complexity of the human race. Travel then becomes a journey of discovery and shared experiences.

Indigenous people and sacred sites

> In some places mass tourism has produced a kind of sub-culture that degrades both the tourists and the host community; it tends to exploit for commercial purposes the traces of "primitive civilizations" and initiation rites still practised in some traditional societies.
>
> John Paul II, 2001

> We are not myths of the past, ruins in the jungle, or zoos. We are people and we want to be respected, not to be victims of intolerance and racism.
>
> Rigoberta Menchu Tum, Mayan

> When the tourists flew in what culture we had
> flew out the window
> we traded our customs for sunglasses and pop
> we turned sacred ceremonies
> into ten-cent peep shows.
>
> Cecil Rajendra, Malaysian poet

In 1988 film-maker Dennis O'Rourke produced a film which has become a classic statement about the clash of cultures to be found in tourism.[14] The documentary shows a group of German tourists as they travel up the Sepik River in Papua New Guinea to view tribal people living in a remote and timeless land. The tourists are on this trip because it gives them the opportunity to have an encounter with people they regard as authentically primitive. The tourists bring with them cameras, videos, money and a host of prejudices about the "noble savage" that demonstrate their ethnocentrism. The film has an added strength from the fact that O'Rourke knows the Sepik area well and is fluent in the language of the local people.

Like many indigenous people, the New Guineans have become consciously aware of their place in the wider modern world and are more rational about it in a Western sense. They know that they have become commodities in the global culture.

The tourists are looking for genuine and untouched traditions which they can record on their cameras to authenticate their travels in a primitive land. The greatest attraction for them is that these tribal people were cannibals in relatively recent times. Although the colonial administration outlawed cannibalism and tribal warfare years ago there are still many of the present New Guineans who lived through the later years of cannibalism and they can speak about their own experience to the visitors.

The New Guineans obligingly put on a stage performance about their early traditions for the benefit of the tourists and then let them dab body paint on their faces. One of the tourists insists he must stand on the actual spot where cannibal acts took place so that he can have his photo taken.

The tourists are anxious to have authentic souvenirs to take home. This is a problem because most of the genuine artefacts have long since disappeared into the museums and collections of foreign countries. Much has also been destroyed. When the missionaries came to the Sepik area they found an active cult based on community spirit houses. As the local people converted to Christianity they were encouraged to remove the carvings and idols and burn them. But the ever resourceful New Guineans can produce modern antiques and the village has revived all the ancient carving arts to provide tourists with the exotic symbols of their past.

Throughout the encounter the tourists show no interest in the actual lives, conflicts and needs of the people from the Sepik River today. Their tour is fixated on a romanticized version of the past which they want to preserve on their videos.

Seen objectively, the film is both tragic and funny. It exposes the superficiality and paternalism of the tourist in contrast to the inner strength and wisdom of the people being visited. Which one is civilized? But the contrast between visitors and locals also exposes the privilege tourists have in being able to exploit the local people to meet their own erroneous understanding of the lost innocence of primitive existence.

The indigenous people of New Guinea are fast losing their distinctive way of life as they make the transition from their traditional ways into the so-called modern Western life-style. Will tourism root them forever in a romantic past or be a catalyst enabling growth and development? These are questions being asked by indigenous people around the world.

The Golden Triangle stands in the mountainous area where Thailand, Myanmar (Burma), China and Laos meet. For the last 100 years this region has been a place of refuge for a diversity of tribes of people who had their origins in Chinese, Burmese or Indian culture. Homeland conflicts forced them to seek a place where they could start life afresh and the Golden Triangle offered them that freedom.

As each new tribe arrived and marked out their territory, they developed their own villages and life-style based on each one's unique culture and traditions. The result was a series of miniature worlds tucked away in the quiet safety of the mountains.

It was only a matter of time before the hill tribes would be discovered by foreigners with an agenda. The first to arrive were missionaries who brought the undoubted advantages of education and modern medicine but who also introduced aspects of Western civilization which quite changed the character of the community.

More recently the hill tribes have been "discovered" again – this time by the tourism industry. The distinctive nature of the various tribes with their colourful costumes, unique dances and customs was a huge attraction to early visitors. As the region became more accessible with good roads and better transport, the hill country became a magnet for tourists. Today all the roads have been upgraded to cater for the daily procession of tourist buses leaving from Chiangrai and Chiangmai. Just as the exotic attraction in New Guinea is cannibalism, here in the Golden Triangle it is opium. While the drug can no longer be grown legally, there are still places where it can be procured and no trip to the mountains is complete without visiting some of the so-called opium warlord's homes.

In addition to the opium stories, visitors are intrigued by the distinctive dress and customs of the various tribes. The Paduangs are a sub-tribe of the Shan, especially distinctive because of the women's practice of placing brass rings around their necks pressing down their shoulders and giving the impression of elongated necks. Other tribes including Karen, Hmong and Lahu have distinctive colourful costumes and unique customs which they will sometimes perform for tourists. The original costumes are incredibly elaborate and require weeks or even months to produce. At one time the women wore their costumes most of the time but today they are only brought out for special occasions. This is partly because the original costumes have been sold to the tourists for prices which seemed high to the tribes people but were a bargain to foreigners. The local people end up at K Mart buying jeans and t-shirts for their family in place of their traditional dress. The village women have turned their talents to making embroidered cushions, clothes and bags for tourists which they tout to visitors or sell at the night markets. Since this is not done in a planned way, disputes often break out between tribals who are trying to sell the same product to the same buyer. The unity which once held tribes together is broken by the competitive consumer society.

Many of the villages in the mountain are in a state of shocking disrepair which forces the discerning tourist to ask who benefits from the tourist dollar. It certainly doesn't appear to be the hill tribe people. Increasing numbers of tribal people are moving to the cities where their limitations of education and language mean they can only undertake menial work. Eventually some of the young people are forced into prostitution.

An additional problem for the half-million hill-tribe people is that they have been denied citizenship rights. That means they do not actually own their land or rights to establish a business. In this disenfranchized situation they have no control over the tourist trade and are forced into a debasing position of powerlessness.

A development group based in the Tribal Museum in Chiangmai received funding from Australia to develop a model village in the hills based on the life of the Akha tribes. Unlike other villages on the hill, there is an entry fee into this village which is administered by the tribal people themselves. The village is certainly in much better condition than other villages on the hill and the protection of the development agency has helped the people regain a certain degree of dignity. But in the end, one leaves the hills with the feeling that people are still being treated as if they are in a ghetto or, as some of them say, creatures in a zoo. There is minimal human relationship between the visitor and the host.

New Guinea and the Golden Triangle are typical examples of hundreds of groups of indigenous people around the planet. These people have the same needs for food and clothing and a fair wage as any of their brothers and sisters in New York or London. In addition, they treasure the traditional way of life which has existed in their community for generations. When tourists come to such places, they bring with them new behavioural patterns and different norms which are both attractive and repulsive. The greater the tourism numbers, the more intense the pressure for change.

There is no easy solution to such encounters but NGOs have been pushing the tourism industry to promote projects which are compatible with the cultural identity of the local population, recognizing their cultural heritage and respecting the cultural integrity of the groups being visited.

In whatever form it comes, tourism is a powerful force which changes the behaviour patterns of communities, especially the habits of the young. When Western foreigners establish a tourist situation in the environment of the third world their presence acts as a catalyst for the transition from traditional ways of life to Western forms of society. Young people especially are attracted by the challenge of the new. The tourism presence may encourage them to reject the norms and customs of the elders which had always given the tribe or community a sense of cohesion and direction. They may begin to regard traditional ways of behaviour as old fashioned and will be attracted by the possessions, wealth, dress and life-style of the tourists.

Pope John Paul II spoke often on tourism matters and issued a warning at the launch of the International Year of Ecotourism that we should not use IYE as a means of distorting ecotourism so that it becomes "a vehicle of abuse and discrimination". His instance of this was "if the protection of the environment were to be made an end in itself, there is a risk that new, modern forms of colonialism will arise that would injure the traditional rights of communities resident in a specific territory". In a subsequent speech he amplified these comments in stronger words:

> Mass tourism is hawking a superficial exoticism that ignores the true culture of destinations. Holiday centres offer a reconstructed ethnicity that satisfies a thirst for new thrills. Tourism has generated a form of sub-culture that humiliates both tourists and the host community.

Whenever tourism moves into traditional indigenous areas it begins to take over the more "exotic" aspects of the culture and adapt them to the demands of the tourist.

Cultural performances, sacred ceremonies and ethnic festivals cease to have their historic and tribal significance and become simply consumer goods which are recycled into a more marketable product. Many cultural performances of indigenous people last for several hours but they have to be squashed down into 10-15 minute slots to provide tourists with an "authentic" experience of their culture.

Indigenous people know that control of their own customs and sacred sites has been taken away from them by foreigners and believe this to be a new form of colonialism which is using them for its own profit. The

International Indigenous Forum on Biodiversity (2004) claimed that "tourism is, with very few exceptions, exploitative and has intensified following the International Year of Ecotourism in 2002. Even our traditional ceremonies and sacred sites are regarded as commodities and niches by the tourism industry."

There have been attempts to protect the use of indigenous presentations in tourism by introducing the principle of prior informed consent by which local people have the right to approve any presentation, determine its form and receive proper recognition of their land rights, customary laws and cultural protocols. But at present, prior consultation rarely takes place in an acceptable form.

Youth hit the tourism scene

> Been there, done that, got the t-shirt.
>
> Hippy tourist

> Travel for the younger set is a part of education; in the elder a part of experience. He that travels into a country before he has some entrance into the language goes to school and not to travel.
>
> Francis Bacon, 1561-1676

The capacity of tourism to pick up thousands of people from various parts of the planet and place them down in the same small area for a week or two is now taken for granted. And as affluence among the young increased and long-distance travel became as simple as a bus ride it was only a matter of time before entrepreneurs started to organize mass gatherings of young people wanting to break the law and ignore social standards in a context where such protest is made possible. The result is that a few tourist destinations have already been turned into what are best described as "rave-centres". The notoriety of these places has given them a kind of star status on young people's television which has contributed to making them even larger and more outrageous each year.

Raves are all-night dance parties for young people. The Europeans were the first to develop the rave but the concept quickly grew and now is found worldwide. A rave is distinguished by exotic venues, hypnotic electronic music and the liberal use of drugs – ecstasy being the current favourite. Though rarely advertised by traditional tourism agents, raves have nevertheless become a large sector of tourism business, especially in Europe and America.

The best-known rave centre, Ibiza, is an island near Majorca off the east coast of Spain. It is a small place with a local population of only 80,000 people but every summer it receives in excess of 1.5 million people, largely from Europe. One section of the island is little more than a collection of night clubs. It has become a magnet for rave tourists, most of whom are under the age of 30 years.

The atmosphere in the clubs is conducive to drug experimentation and in some bars class A drugs like cocaine or "crystal meth" can be bought over the counter as part of the "drinks promotions" offered to holiday punters. Huge nightclubs cater for crowds of up to 10,000 people and many of them open at midnight and remain open until 9 a.m. the next morning.

The pervasive drug culture leads to an open sexual scene. Mark Bellis of Liverpool's John Moores University was the leader of a survey of 1500 young people which showed that 54 percent of young tourists in Ibiza had at least one sexual partner on the island. Some of these partners were their regular sexual partner who went with them on holiday. Nearly a quarter (23 percent) of people had more than one sexual partner on the island.[15]

Bellis noted that the mission statement for Club 18-30, one of the larger tourist agents for young British people to Ibiza, promotes their product in these words: "Try sex in the surf; wake up in the wrong hotel; drink all your duty free in one day."

In 2003, health authorities on Ibiza said they could no longer cope with the number of Britons being admitted to hospital because of drug abuse. In one season they dealt with 260 cases ranging from overdoses to withdrawal symptoms. A further 500 young people were admitted to accident and emergency after being injured through drink- or drug-related incidents.

Ibiza gets international exposure through a number of prurient television programmes which exaggerate the wonderful happiness and freedom of Ibiza but carefully avoid giving exposure to the negative aspects of their impact on Ibiza or themselves.

A growing number of rave centres similar to Ibiza are developing around the world. In Southern Thailand, when the full moon dawns over Haad Rin Beach, up to 40,000 young tourists mainly from America and Europe hold a one night mega-rave over one-kilometre of beach at which they consume gallons of alcohol, take psychoactive drugs, dance, smoke, vomit, have sex and collapse on the sand as dawn comes.

Tourism has always had the capacity to give individuals the chance to escape from the normal restraints of their home into an environment in which the individual is able to indulge in behaviour which would not be acceptable or lawful in their own country. The youth rave scenes where the excessive use of illegal drugs, criminal activities and promiscuity is the norm carry this feature of tourism to a worrying conclusion.

Sex tourism

> A tourist has temporarily resigned from real life and feels free to do what he wants in a land where nobody knows him.
>
> Dr Nitthi Siriwong, Thai social historian

> There is only one man in the world
> and his name is All Men.
> There is only one woman in the world
> and her name is All Women.
> There is only one child in the world
> and the child's name is All Children.
>
> Carl Sandburg, The *Family of Man*, 1955

From earliest days, travel and sex have gone together. In the ruins of the ancient city of Ephesus or in Pompeii, tourists today are shown the buildings which once housed the region's largest collection of brothels. Prostitution has always flourished in seaports where travellers and seamen were to be found.

A Japanese proverb explains this phenomena. It says that "the traveller knows no shame". You don't have to go to Ibiza to realize the truth of this statement. The further one travels away from home, the greater the temptation to act in a way that would never be contemplated when living in the restraints of one's own home town. Travellers who would never enter a red-light massage parlour or casino in their home town seem quite willing to do so in Bangkok or Las Vegas. The normal restraints which would prevent a person taking drugs are lifted when that person is travelling in those parts of the world where drugs are freely available and acceptable. For some people, the further they travel from home, the less moral they become.

With the passing of time, this human trait has been increasingly commercialized and today sex tourism is a major industry. The use of the term "sex tourism" probably originated in Japan in the 1970s when women activists mounted a campaign against the growing practice of companies sending their employees to other parts of Asia on paid holidays in which a major component was organized sexual experiences. The term gained international recognition at a tourism conference in Manila organized by the Christian Conference of Asia in 1980.

While there will be continuing debate about the morality of prostitution, there is one aspect of it which has always been seen as abhorrent and that is when prostitution forces the person into slavery. When women are forced into the sex industry through poverty or by criminal action, prostitution becomes unacceptable by any law or any standard.

In the past decade the world has become aware of another, and even more insidious, aspect of prostitution slavery and that is the enslavement of children to act as prostitutes. In 1989 an Asian-based church body, the Ecumenical Coalition on Third World Tourism (ECTWT), conducted research in a number of Asian countries and brought the findings to a conference held in Chiangmai in May 1990. The research uncovered the astonishing reality of an active and extensive international trade in children which had developed in the region. The studies indicated that up to one million children under the age of 16 years were in sexual slavery in Asia alone.[16] Although many of these children were serving a local demand, there appeared to be a surprisingly large number of foreign tourists who were travelling to certain countries in Asia solely to have sex with children.

Around the same time, a number of public events took place in Southeast Asia which reinforced the seriousness of what was happening.

- Firemen entered a Thai brothel after a fire in 1984 and found the burnt bodies of five young girls trapped in a cellar because they were chained to their beds. They had been kept in slavery to work as child prostitutes.
- In 1991 a public trial in Manila revealed that an Austrian tourist, Dr Ritter, had been sexually abusing children in Olongapo. A young street girl called Rosario was so badly abused by the tourist that she died a terrible and painful death.
- In Bangkok a young American Mormon tourist, Mark Morgan, appeared so concerned about street children that he opened a shelter for young boys in Bangkok and another in Northern Thailand. American Mormons put money into the project until it was found that Morgan was a convicted and well-known paedophile who was using the shelters to provide sexual partners for other American paedophiles. Morgan and his associates were arrested and imprisoned in 1989.

With all this publicity, the situation of children kept as sexual slaves for tourists could no longer be hidden or tolerated and those who attended the Chiangmai conference held discussions on ways to raise public concern about the abuse of such a large number of children. The result was the formation of an international organization aimed at ending the prostitution of children in Asia. Formed in 1991, ECPAT (End Child Prostitution in Asian Tourism) was founded as an organization which sought to educate the public on what was taking place and lobby for change with governments and the civil society. It was the first significant voice to be heard denouncing the trade in children for sexual purposes.

In the space of a few short years the organization out-grew its Christian origin to become open to all religions; it developed beyond its Asian roots to become fully international; it went beyond the narrow focus on tourism to deal with other social activities and it expanded its work from children in prostitution to include related issues such as pornography and child-trafficking. Today, ECPAT International (End Child Prostitution, Child Pornography and Trafficking in Children for Sexual Purposes) is now operating in 69 countries around the world. Partly as a consequence of the work of ECPAT over the last 15 years, the world has become much more aware of the size and significance of child sex tourism.

Paedophiles and other abusers who travel are now unlikely to be part of organized sex tours but instead will use the internet and share information with other abusers to seek out places to visit and obtain data on the availability of children. The worldwide attention given to child sex tourism has made persistent offenders more circumspect. Organizations monitoring the movement of the trade in children note that as one country improves its laws or gains more publicity, abusive tourists are soon made aware of what has happened and move to new areas. In Asia, for example, the focus on Thailand as a child sex tourist destination has seen the criminals who control the trade move much of their activity to new areas such as Cambodia where laws are more lax and where law enforcement officers can sometimes be bribed. Similar movements have been noted in child sex destinations in Eastern Europe and Central America.

After a rather shaky start, the tourism industry has itself begun to be much more proactive in trying to protect children who are the victims of prostitution. It has been made clear that tourism itself is not to blame for the rise in child sex tourism but, since it is the context in which such abuse takes place, it can play a strategic role in monitoring offenders and helping to protect children.

There are several instances of the way the tourism industry is responding. The Universal Federation of Travel Agents Association (UFTAA), a huge network of tourist agents, went public on the issue as early as 1993. Thanks in part to the passion of one of its leaders, UFTAA urged its members to adopt a "Children's and Travel Agents' Charter" through which the industry would protect children. Soon after, in 1996, the World Tourism Organization adopted a statement on the prevention of organized sex tourism and set up an active task force as part of its move to introduce and monitor a broad code of ethics for tourism. Most other international tourism organizations have adopted professional codes or other self-regulatory measures to stop sexual exploitation in tourism.

Beyond these international initiatives, tourism workers on the ground discovered that their greatest contribution to helping children could be in the countries where child sex tourism was found. Hotel workers were seen as key figures because they can usually deduce what is happening in their hotel and alert the authorities. This has led some of the major hotel chains to introduce training schemes for their staff so that they will monitor possible illegal activities with children in their hotels. A significant example of this is the giant ACCOR chain of hotels which has 3800 hotels in 90 countries. The company has entered into an agreement with ECPAT International "to raise awareness and educate both guests and employees" regarding child sexual tourism. Over three months, from October 2002 to January 2003, ACCOR and the ECPAT-related Childwise Tourism ran major tourism awareness programmes for 1422 of its staff in Asia. Through ACCOR travel agencies more than one million leaflets warning against child sex tourism have been included with travel tickets. A number of other hotels and travel agencies have taken similar action and instituted measures to prevent tourists using their privileged position to commit crimes against children.

The size of the problem should not be underestimated. UNICEF believes that 1.2 million children are sold into sexual slavery every year and 2 million children – mainly girls, but also a significant number of boys – are believed to be part of the multibillion-dollar commercial sex trade.[17] In earlier years, children were openly for sale in a number of the traditional tourism destinations but with educational programmes and tougher sentencing the trade in children has become less obvious and hopefully less available.

The criminals who control the trade in children realized that there would be advantages in having children who have been trafficked from another country. These children often cannot speak the local language nor do they have official papers and in this situation of dependency they can be exploited as slaves. The prostitution of children has therefore encouraged considerable movement from country to country. Tourism routes provide an umbrella under which many of these children are being trafficked. For example, between 5000 and 7000 girls are trafficked across the border from Nepal to India each year. Most of them end up in the sex trade and a large number come as part of a tourist "family" with false documentation. In countries where border crossings have been relaxed or even eradicated in the interests of tourism, the movement of children appears to have increased. The difficulty of monitoring child trafficking has been noted in Europe as children from Eastern Europe are abducted to work in various countries in the West.

Efforts to end the sexual exploitation of children now receive strong backing from many sectors of the tourism industry. A code of conduct has been developed through which major tourism agencies sign an agreement with ECPAT International to work to overcome the existence of child sex tourism.

The World Tourism Organization has more recently developed a global code of ethics in which they state, "The exploitation of human beings in any form, particularly sexual and especially when applied to children, conflicts with the fundamental aims of tourism and is the negation of tourism."[18]

Human rights

In recent years repressive political regimes have sometimes turned to tourism to try and portray a flattering picture of their country. Even the most tyrannical leaders need to be concerned about their international image, so tourism is a wonderful gift. It feeds on dreams and images and with a little engineering a repressed country can be dressed up to give visitors the illusion of goodness and freedom.

Under President Marcos, the Philippines used this manipulation to its fullest. What is more, Marcos was quite unashamed of announcing his intention. Philippine tourism officials speaking to a church conference in 1980 openly stated that President Marcos had a bad image in the Western press because of his policy of martial law so tourism was seen by the president as an opportunity to improve this image. In an action that had no precedent up to that time, the Philippine government laid out several hundred million dollars to subsidize the building of 14 luxury hotels along the Manila waterfront. This was rushed through in time for meetings of the World Bank in Manila in 1976. Exceptionally generous tax exemptions and direct financial contributions enabled the world's leading hotel chains to establish themselves in the city at very little cost.

These actions gave the Philippines the largest number of 5-star hotels of any city in Asia but the gloss of the new hotels could not hide the dross of the poverty and repression in the rest of the country so tourism failed to take off. By 1980 most of the hotels were facing annual losses of several million dollars.

With the help of Imelda Marcos, more money was pumped into subsidizing prestige events such as an international film event and numerous international conferences, but the media continued to expose the sham of this kind of tourism and hotel occupancy remained disturbingly low. In the same year as the Marcos government put $300 million into tourism projects the government spent less than 15 million dollars on housing and public buildings.

There were some travel writers innocent enough to be influenced by the propaganda. A writer for *Travel Trade Gazette* welcomed martial law in the Philippines and encouraged people to visit the new Philippines. Under Marcos, he wrote "the tourism industry has undergone a great change. It has become purposeful. It has received government support." The writer said that martial law was "benevolent" and concluded "trees have been planted everywhere and private armies have been abolished".[19]

Perhaps he had been deceived by the huge hoardings which stretched for several kilometres along the highway from the airport to the hotels, erected to hide the most appalling slums. Had he looked behind the signs and seen the shocking poverty it might have given the lie to his belief that this was a happy and prosperous country for tourists to visit.

Other dictators in recent years have attempted to use tourism to justify or to hide their dictatorship. This is true whether they are right-wing like Papa Doc Duvalier in Haiti or left-wing like Fidel Castro in Cuba. In the politics of both capitalism and communism, tourism can be used as an excuse for muffling opposition and domesticating discontent.

On the contemporary political scene, activists have been distressed at the brazen way the Burmese government has attempted to use tourism to bolster its illegal regime. Burma (Myanmar) has one of the most repressive governments in the world. The country is ruled by a brutal military dictatorship which is charged by the United Nations with a "crime against humanity" for its systematic abuses of human rights. It has refused to hand over power to the party which won a legitimate election and has placed the leader of the party, Nobel Peace Laureate Aung San Suu Kyi, under house arrest.

The dictatorship turned to tourism in a blatant attempt to regain international favour and to obtain needed overseas funds. The way it went about developing the necessary tourist infrastructure was an outrage to its own people. Using its dictatorial powers and state control of the economy, the needed work was done by evicting people from their homes and using forced labour. Reports tell of men, women, children and the elderly being forced to work under harsh conditions on roads, railways and tourism projects.

The regime in Rangoon claims that 656,910 tourists visited Burma in 2004 with 240,000 coming by air but statistics used by the Burmese government are notoriously unreliable and observers believe the tourism figures are inflated by including trades people crossing the border on a day trip. To meet its ambitious targets the government is now saying it will expand Rangoon airport to handle 2.3 million visitors by 2006.

When Burma launched its campaign to increase tourism through "Visit Myanmar Year", it sparked off a debate about the ethics of such a move. Surprisingly, one of the authors of a Lonely Planet guidebook published an article in the Bangkok newspaper *The Nation* titled "Why Tourism Helps Democracy in Burma". He argued that tourism would help ordinary people and not just the generals. Lonely Planet has had a good record in dealing with some of the negative issues in tourism and the article brought worldwide reaction, with the Burma Campaign UK and Tourism Concern leading a boycott against Lonely Planet publications. The argument that boosting tourism will help ordinary people who suffer under repressive regimes simply cannot be sustained. It is the essence of dictatorships that the rulers have no interest in the democratic rights of ordinary people and will simply use them as pawns to expand their own power. Tourism to such countries is a mechanism which can be used to justify further repressive acts against the people.

Aung San Suu Kyi herself supported a tourism boycott of Burma, stating that "tourism has its good and bad sides, that I hardly need to say. But Visit Myanmar Year 1996 we do not support, because this is just a big political propaganda campaign."[20] In a situation such as Burma the issue of tourism cannot be debated in terms of economics alone but reflects the need of an unpopular ruling elite to give legitimacy to a regime that has no legitimacy among its own people.

6. A Tourism Which Is Economically Just and Viable

> What's gone wrong with tourism is that the age-old balance between host and guest has tipped too far in favour of the guest.
>
> Alison Stancliffe, co-founder of Tourism Concern, UK

In the 1970s and 1980s when mass tourism was being promoted among poor countries it was introduced in a rush with little regard for either the environment or the rights of the people. The illusion of benign foreign investment helping the country encouraged governments to cut corners and give exemptions to foreign investors in the hope that eventually the money would trickle down to the community. In fact, the continuing result of much of this investment was that a few local leaders became rich from kickbacks and concessions while most people were in a worse economic situation post-tourism than pre-tourism.

Thailand is a typical instance of a country which today has become a major tourism destination but which gave up everything to develop its tourism in early years. When the initial boom collapsed with a financial crisis in 1997, the full extent of the disaster was recognized. A leading newspaper in Bangkok summed up the way tourism had created problems in the country.

> It (tourism) contributed heavily to widespread land speculation, excessive promotion of hotels which led to massive glut, and abuse of the environment and the rights of small landholders by unscrupulous investors. The eagerness to promote tourism also meant a worsening of Thai society through prostitution and narcotics. State agencies joined the bandwagon to try, for example, to open up national parks with little concern for (the ecology).[21]

The country continues to struggle with the consequences of these actions.

When all the factors are added together how well does tourism improve the economy of a poor country?

Leakage

> Tourism activists increasingly view commercial tourism as a modern day social and economic distortion requiring radical and urgent reconstruction.
>
> Dr Ahn Jae Wong, Christian Conference of Asia

The critical question which developing countries face is how much of the income generated by tourism remains in the country and how much leaks out to overseas investors. This leakage is hotly debated by economists and tourism proponents throughout the world and is a source of debate whenever developing countries decide to give priority to tourism development.

The issue can be stated in a simple illustration. The mythical island state of Motu is pressured by intergovernmental organizations to develop a tourism industry as a means of attracting foreign currency and providing employment for its people. The politicians on Motu are impressed and make the decision to give tourism national priority. That resolution leads to a number of immediate initiatives. Foreign capital must be secured in order to develop the infrastructure in such things as roading, airports and sewage disposal. A soft loan is organized from the same intergovernmental agency that floated the original idea. With help from overseas experts, Motu then sets out to encourage developers who will invest in new projects and construct hotels, resorts, golf courses and other auxiliary services. These also come at a price and to protect their investment, the developers will extract concessions, including the right to retain the management and ownership of their properties.

The expansion of Motu's airport to be able to accept large jet planes has been costly but with help from the international community at least one airline has provisionally agreed to include the country in its flight schedules.

By this time Motu has already built up a large debt and is hoping for quick recovery of some of the promised benefits. But the tourism market is both fickle and competitive and tourists are used to shopping around for the best deal. Motu is a new destination and as such it has novelty value but tourism agents will have to work very hard to get it on the international map. In order to do this they will rely on cheap prices, small profit margins and special concessions. It will be a long time before Motu begins to reduce much of its debt.

Look now at a group of tourists travelling to Motu. This first group comes from Japan. They arrive and will depart on a Japanese airline, staying at a Japanese owned hotel, looked after by Japanese guides driving a Japanese bus. When they have meals they want to enjoy their own food. That requires Motu using its foreign currency to import barrels of sake and premium whisky as well as the other foods which are distinctive to the Japanese diet.

But it doesn't end there. American tourists are also coming to the island so a hamburger chain has been opened and they are importing their potatoes from Idaho and the beef from Australia. Motu finds itself trapped in a situation where it has only a handful of factories and few cottage industries so almost all the requirements of the tourists have to be imported. In simple terms, this is the story of leakage for Motu.

While the general problem can be stated in an understandable way and is evident from anyone's observation, there is a maze of complexity once we begin to explore the detail. It would be helpful if we could produce definitive research figures to illustrate the point but even a partial summary of the studies done would require several books. The results from all this research seems to depend partly on whether it is being done by the tourism industry, a UN agency or for an independent organization. Obviously, it is also dependent on which country or region is being considered and what type of tourism is under scrutiny.

If we consider cruise ships for example, a small island gets virtually no return when it invests in port facilities and tourism programmes for visiting ships. The largest concentration of cruise ships is found in the Caribbean (44.5 percent of the world's cruise passengers) and many of them encourage their passengers to spend their time and money on board. When they stop at a port, opportunities to go sight-seeing are closely managed and restricted. Local entrepreneurs developing a local project aimed at the tourism market are unlikely to profit from the passing ships.

It is a similar problem with group tours. The United Nations Environmental Programme estimates that in all-inclusive package tours around 80 percent of the tourist expenditure goes to airlines, hotels and other international companies, most of which will be located in the travellers' home country. Very little goes to local businesses or workers and even then some of their income will also disappear through leakage.[22]

Figures from studies are like scatter guns. However, UNCTAD (United Nations Committee on Trade and Development) bit the bullet and made the claim that from each US$100 spent on a vacation tour by a tourist from a developed country, only around US$5 actually stays in a developing-country destination's economy. They claimed further that the average import-related leakage for most developing countries today is between 40 percent and 50 percent of gross tourism earnings for small economies and between 10 percent and 20 percent for most advanced and diversified economies.[23]

There were claims that ecotourism would change this situation and bring more benefit to developing countries. To test this possibility, a comprehensive study on a major ecotourism project in Taman Negara, a national park in western Malaysia, was commissioned by a German government agency in 1997. It concluded that only a tiny proportion of the tourist money actually reaches ecotourism destinations in the country being visited. The author of the study looked at the expenditure of European and North American ecotourists and found that about two-thirds of the expenditure goes to foreign airlines and travel agencies and a large proportion of the rest is spent, both before and after the visit to an ecotourism destination, in the large cities and well-established tourist centres.[24]

Calling a tourism project eco-friendly may not make much difference to its economic impact. The amount of leakage appears to depend greatly on the nature of the local economy and the ability of local authorities to keep pressure on tourism developers to ensure that local inputs are purchased for their projects. NGOs have argued that by devising local training programmes and establishing educational projects, the tourism industry could ensure that qualified local people are employed in their projects. By training local people instead of foreigners to become guides, the tourist would benefit from local knowledge and the community as a whole would be enriched. Incentives are also needed so that local people can develop small and medium-sized tourism enterprises such as accommodation which would have less impact on the environment.[25] These changes would be beneficial but even so the situation will always be tilted in favour of overseas investors and the owners of large hotels and resorts.

It is this economic strength of foreign developers that explains why small islands or regions which have invested heavily in tourism for decades are still unable to see much improvement in their country's overall economy or their individual wealth.

Who benefits?

> We have allowed the tourists to turn back into a barbarian past. Grabbing and consuming uncritically all that is put before them by an industry that is led by numbers and targets.
>
> Nina Rao, India

Crucial to any discussion of tourism in developing countries is the effect it has on the local people. Do they really benefit from a tourism development?

The argument in favour of tourism in such countries has always been that it will provide employment for the locals and that growth in income will consequently raise the standard of living. As with so many issues surrounding tourism, the answer to such arguments is always mixed and most will end in "yes – but". It is clearly true, for example, that tourism will bring more jobs. Yes – but most of the jobs are menial and low paid, including servant roles to foreigners and prostitution. It is also true that tourism brings more money into the country. Yes – but the arrival of tourism also sends the prices higher and local people struggle to survive in the newly inflated economy. The arguments go on.

Look at the way it happened in our mythical island state of Motu. Over centuries the island had developed a rather complicated social system in which all members knew their place. The council of chiefs looked after any disputes that arose and maintained order between the families and sub-tribes that made up the population. With a combination of fishing, chickens and crops the island was self-sufficient and even when a cyclone struck the people managed to survive by sharing resources and cooperation. Were they happy? Yes and no. Like people everywhere they knew how to celebrate the happy times and sometimes wished that their life could be better. Largely isolated from the world, life went by at a predictable pace and in a manner that everyone understood. If that spells happiness, that is what they had.

When tourism came to Motu things changed dramatically. There was an immediate demand for workers but regrettably the island people had not developed any of the skills needed to build airports and hotels except to provide muscle for the labouring tasks. This meant the developers had to fly in large numbers of engineers, designers and a dozen different kinds of tradespeople.

The presence of such a large number of foreigners had a profound effect on the character of Motu. Young people were the first to sign up for the labouring tasks and in doing so they came in contact with a different world which had an excitement and variety that they had never known. They were attracted to the life-style of these workers from another country and began to copy their habits and speech.

Meanwhile, the older members of Motu were struggling to come to terms with other problems brought by the foreigners. With so many additional people on the island, food and drink had to be imported in large quantities. The newcomers had deep pockets and were happy to pay higher prices for their goods. The laws of supply and demand inevitably pushed up prices and soon the local people were having difficulty in paying their food bills. The old values of sharing and self-help were rapidly disappearing. When the people complained, some of the chiefs tried to reassure them by saying that all these workers will soon be gone and then the tourists will come and make us rich.

Nothing, it seemed, could stop the heavy machinery of development rolling on. A hill that was sacred to the island tribes was bulldozed out of existence without any genuine discussion. The planners had shown a small group of local chiefs a map of their intended actions but there was no common language to communicate the intention of the plan, and given that it was the first map the chiefs had seen it was not a very effective consultation. When the community discovered what had happened there was weeping and grief that lasted for several days. The developers apologised and gave a great feast as compensation, but it was too late. The sacred site had gone forever.

For the first time, sharp divisions began to appear between families and generations and the unity which had been a mark of the social fabric of Motu was in the process of disintegration. Older people on the island blamed the newcomers for their problems. These new workers dressed and spoke and acted in a way that was not appropriate. They had no appreciation for the local customs and treated the chiefs, the old people and the women with little respect. Worst of all, they seemed to be influencing the young people who were listening to the foreigners instead to their own elders.

Eventually, the hotels and airport were completed and the tourists began to arrive but it was not the economic windfall the chiefs had expected. The administrative jobs in tourism were all occupied by foreigners who brought their own set of values and rules to the position. Local men gave up their fishing to work in the hotels on menial tasks. And as the cost of goods continued to rise, some of the women had to resort to prostitution to gain enough money to survive. When families could not cope, children were sent to the beaches to beg for money from the tourists.

In time, the young people from Motu will possibly be trained to occupy positions of leadership in the tourism industry. But by then the island of Motu may well have metamorphosed into a pseudo-Western society, with the locals maintaining a swept-up version of their traditional customs and costumes primarily in order to present a performance for the tourists in their hotel.

You will hear echoes of Motu in other places in the world. When small self-contained regions or islands are selected as prime tourist destinations the whole character of the community changes. The "blessings" of "Western civilized modernity" are brought in and superimposed on top of a very simple and ancient traditional society. The clash of cultures is inevitable and there is usually only one winner.

We must also recognize that there are many people in our world who claim that when these changes occur in a developing country it is a good thing. They will argue that societies which the affluent world regard as primitive need to be brought into the modern world. Creating a tourism market in an underdeveloped country, they believe, is the best way to bring to the natives the gifts of democracy, affluence and modernization.

The effect of such thinking is to make tourism a new colonialism, spreading the good news of affluence and consumerism to the remote corners of the world, repeating the old colonialist arguments in modern dress.

The imposition of foreign values is a controversy the church has long debated. In the early years of its missionary history the church saw no contradiction in mixing up the blessings of Western civilization with the message of the Christian gospel. The historical experiences of the churches should bring us to at least one clear conclusion and that is that one dominant culture cannot/should not impose its own cultural and social values on another culture without that second culture having a full understanding and acceptance of what such imposition will mean.

If we translate that philosophy into the tourism situation it means that tourism should not be imposed; it has to be accepted. The summary of this conclusion in contemporary society suggests that any country or region which becomes a tourism destination the local people must:

a) have a proper understanding of what is proposed;
b) become complete partners in the management of the tourism development;
c) be full beneficiaries of the benefits which come from the project.

Anything less than this is a re-hashing of the worst features of colonialism.

Seeking an economic miracle

> The travel and tourism industry "is essentially the renting out for short-term lets of other people's environments.
>
> Lord Marshall, British Airways, 1994

Tourism is constantly being heralded as an ideal route to economic independence for struggling countries, islands, cities or regions. It is a tempting package and sometimes it can be successful. But the reality is there are risks and there will be dramatic failures. When tourism is given priority ahead of all other forms of economic development the country's economy becomes particularly vulnerable to external pressures. Tourism is a fickle industry and recent years have shown a spate of instances where the tourism dream has not brought the expected benefit to the local people. Some examples:

1. The Maldives

The World Tourism Organization maintains figures on the size of the tourism workforce and the top of their range is in the Maldives where an incredible 83 percent of the Maldive workforce are employed in tourism. While such a large number of people working should indicate a wealthy workforce, the facts are depressing. Reports claim that nearly half of the local population are living on US$1.17 per day with 22 percent living on well below US$1 which, according to international standards, means they are living in poverty.[26]

A United Nations study recently found that 30 percent of Maldivian children under 5 are suffering from malnutrition, a situation as acute as sub-Saharan Africa. The cause appears to be that fresh fruit and vegetables go directly to the tourism resorts, bypassing the local people. Not only has tourism failed to deliver any golden egg to the Maldives, its people face a doubtful future after the great tsunami of December 2004 swept over the islands and destroyed much of the people's habitat.

2. The Seychelles

The Seychelles is an independent island group off the coast of Africa which made a commitment to tourism and opened an international airport in 1970. The country developed a strong tourism sector employing more than 20 percent of the island workforce. The success of the venture encouraged developers to open luxury resorts but the isolation of the Seychelles became its enemy. In July 2003 the whole industry suffered a crisis when British Airways – the only carrier to the country with first class seats – decided to pull out of this route. The airline said it was cutting its flights from London to Seychelles so that it could utilize its planes more efficiently. Tourism numbers have dropped significantly and hotels struggle with occupancy.

3. The Dominican Republic

Even when a country is successful in attracting tourists, tourism does not always benefit the mass of the population. The Dominican Republic is the most popular tourist destination in the Caribbean, claiming to have the largest all-inclusive resort industry in the world with 50,000 rooms. Although it had the highest economic growth in the Americas from 1996-2000, 90 percent of the 8 million residents in the country live below the poverty line.[27]

4. Benidorm

Benidorm is a popular tourist resort city on the coast of Spain with more than 130 hotels. Dry almost all year round, the centre depends on extracting water from underground for use in its 30,000 swimming pools, golf courses and hotels. As the level of the underground water drops, seawater creeps in, poisoning the surrounding farmland. Water is being removed from aquifers up to three times faster than it can be replenished. A single golf course in the area consumes as much water as a town of 10,000 people in the area.[28]

5. Venice

Venice is losing its population. In the 1950s it had a population of 175,000 but today there are less than 40,000 living in the city. In winter the town goes to sleep, with empty streets and few people. It awakes again in summer with up to 15 million tourists packing its narrow lanes. Specializing in tourism alone has its negative aspects in Venice.

A UNESCO report says that "paradoxically, tourists are drawn by an image which is destroyed by their very presence, since at peak times the huge crowds produce congestion which destroys the original atmosphere of the city". The influx of tourists adds to the array of water and noise pollution problems. In summer, the narrow canals are congested with motorized boats and gondolas fighting for canal space.The American novelist Mary McCarthy once remarked, "The tourist Venice is Venice – a folding picture-postcard of itself."

6. Tenerife, Canary Islands

Mass tourism is the driving force behind the Canary Islands' economy. It has created a host of environmental problems. Water is in short supply, with underground aquifers unable to cope with the demand from swimming pools and golf courses. Unregulated poor quality housing has led to a ruined environment and attracts the wrong kind of tourist. A report in July 2004 claimed that tourism in the capital Tenerife had plummeted by 19 percent.[29]

7. Bermuda

Bermuda is one of the most densely populated areas of the world, with 64,000 people crowded into a small island just 21 square miles in area. The country was once the pace-setter in international tourism but this was hard to sustain in such a small territory. Now the local industry is in the doldrums, with fewer tourists travelling to Bermuda. Visitor arrivals dropped by more than 20 percent in the year 2001 and severely again the following year after the terrorist attack on the New York Twin Towers. Tourism leaders blame the decline on intense competition from countries all over the world. Bermuda, they claim, is now struggling to keep up.

7. The Great Tsunami and Tourism

> If tourism is supposed to alleviate poverty, how come so many of the communities which were devastated were living in poverty despite being in some of the most popular tourism destinations in the world?
>
> Tourist in Phuket, quoted in *Tourism Concern)*

> Tourists are the modern rapists of paradise, and if one positive thing could possibly come from the tsunami it would be the rebuilding of local economies so that they are self-sufficient.
>
> Janet Steet-Porter, *The Independent*, January 2005

December 2004 and a devastating tsunami roared into areas of Southeast Asia, leaving behind a trail of destruction and killing an unknown number of people estimated to be in excess of 250,000. Such events are not uncommon in Asia. In 1970, a cyclone followed by a storm surge is believed to have killed more than 500,000 Bengalis (official estimates were 300,000). In both China and Bangladesh floods, famine and earthquakes regularly kill more than a quarter of a million people and leave millions homeless.

Normally when such disasters strike, the world's media record shocking images of destruction, a few governments pledge aid to the stricken communities and in a few weeks the whole event is forgotten by the media. A Hollywood divorce in the USA or a politician's adultery in Britain has greater news value to Western media than attempts to rehabilitate the lives of a million Asian victims.

But when the tsunami hit Southeast Asia in 2004 things were different. The world's media descended on the area en masse and for weeks following television and newspaper stories were dominated by an event which some media people were wrongly describing as the worst natural disaster in a century. Heads of state declared days of mourning and numerous countries were fired by a burst of generosity which led to governments allocating unprecedented sums of money for rehabilitation. For a few days it had all the appearance of an auction, with each country bidding more to prove their generosity.

The tsunami was a terrible tragedy but the subsequent reaction raises significant questions. Why were governments willing to pledge huge sums of money for this particular event when previous tragedies had not elicited the same response? And with so many resources available in the world, why is it that when disaster strikes poor people continue to be dependent on the charity of celebrities and the patronage of foreign governments to provide money for their survival?

Such questions raise broad issues affecting the whole structure of society but there is one specific fact which relates to the theme of this book. Why is it that this tsunami produced a huge charitable response from all around the world, when greater disasters in China, Rwanda and India have not? And the answer is clear: it was the presence of tourists from several affluent countries who were killed or wounded by the tsunami that gave the tragedy such importance in the world's media and led to the huge international response.

A cynic could well ask: How many Asians equal one American? (or how many Africans equal one German, etc.). As Nelson Mandela pointed out, more people die each week through poverty than were killed in the tsunami.

The tsunami was news because of the tourists. European and American tourists flock to Southeast Asia in December to flee the winter cold in their own countries. Each year there is a growing influx of tourists making the coasts of Thailand and Sri Lanka their chief holiday destination. Costs are incredibly low in comparison with European resorts and for some tourists the ready availability of cheap sex is an attraction they do not know in their own country.

Many tourists who perished in the tsunami were living in simple accommodation that sat right on the beachfront so there was no escape from the power of the water. Their deaths help to highlight the destruction of the foreshore which has taken place in tourism beach destinations. Mangrove forests and coral reefs which have been a traditional buffer against the power of a tsunami have gone. Resort developers have been permitted to have absolute beach frontage and have altered the beach landscape according to their own designs. The weakness of local regulations has given developers and local entrepreneurs the opportunity to act with impunity.

Unfortunately, the lessons of the tsunami will not be heeded and the same mistakes will be repeated. In the wake of the flood waters, developers have immediately moved into the devastated lands. Typical is the case of the Baan Khao Lak fishing village which the tsunami completely destroyed. The village sits on an idyllic small beach and has been the home of 14 large families who have lived in the same area for generations. When the waters receded and the surviving members of the village returned, they found that developers had already moved in, put up fences and staked a claim for the land. Without any written title, the families are faced with the probability that they are now homeless, jobless and landless. Baan Khao is just one of 32 villages in this area facing the same fate.

It is a lax legal system that permits such things to happen but it is the influence and the greed of tourism developers that uses a tragedy such as the tsunami to further exploit the poor.

8. Tourism and the Church

I have seen many things in my travels, and I understand more than I can express.

Ecclesiasticus 34:11

In the middle ages, people were tourists because of religion, whereas now they are tourists because tourism is their religion.

Robert Runcie, Archbishop of Canterbury 1980-1990

In 1937 the League of Nations first used the term tourism, with "tourist" defined as "people travelling abroad for periods of over 24 hours". On that definition, Christians have been tourists for 2000 years and it has been an important part of their religious experience. Originally their journeys were called pilgrimages and took them to places of religious importance such as the Holy Land or famous shrines with relics of the saints. In this respect Christians were no different from the other world religions in which journeys to holy places such as Benares (Hindu), Mecca (Muslim) or Angkor Wat (Buddhist) were a significant part of religious life.

In the 19th and 20th century, Christians began to travel with a new sense of purpose – this time as a part of their duty to win converts in every corner of the globe. This missionary movement emanated primarily from Europe and was largely carried along by the colonial world-view of the time. One of its greatest effects was to open up remote areas of the world to the influence of modernity and expose them to new and foreign ideas of which the Christian faith was one.

During the 20th century, Christians were joined by a new breed of travellers who "travelled for the purpose of recreation" (official definition of tourist used by the World Tourism Organization). The number of these new travellers started to multiply at an astonishing rate and their activity soon became one of the most important social developments of the late 20th century. In a few places, the church started to take notice.

In 1967, the first international conference on tourism was convened by the World Council of Churches in Tutzing, Germany. It was a rather confusing event, initiated in large part by American Christians working in national parks whose primary interest in tourism was to use it as a means of evangelism.

It was left to Christians in the third world to raise questions about justice and the role of tourism in society. The call came first from small island states in the Caribbean and Asia where there was concern about the way tourism was changing the customs and family values of their countries. In 1975 the Christian Conference of Asia initiated a research programme in the three island territories of Hong Kong, Penang and Bali where Christian groups were struggling to make sense of the tourist invasion. Researchers described tourism as a dilemma and could not decide whether it was good or bad. This meeting was followed by a much larger conference in 1980 at which 18 Asia-Pacific countries were present. The conclusion this time was more emphatic. It was recognized that tourism had the potential to benefit society but the way it has been used in many countries, "tourism wreaked more havoc than brought benefits to recipient third-world countries".[30]

Out of all this debate there emerged a new organization called the Ecumenical Coalition on Third World Tourism (now known as the Ecumenical Coalition on Tourism – ECOT). For almost 25 years this organization has been the international voice for Christian concern about tourism. More recently it was nominated by the World Social Forum to be the focal point for other world agencies in order to "change the character of tourism towards a tourism that is just and equitable for people in all situations".

Partly as a result of these international initiatives a number of national churches and church agencies have developed tourism-related programmes which have emerged from specific local situations.

In tourist-sending countries there has been little church attention on the issue except for a few tourist-focused programmes educating the traveller on how to act in a foreign land. In this regard the German churches have been, by far, the most effective in demonstrating the importance of tourism to the churches. Thanks to substantial funding from churches, the agency which is today called Tourism Watch has developed extensive links with both the tourism industry and the churches and has exerted a positive influence on the development of a more responsible German tourism.

Since its establishment in 1975 the German agency has maintained a professional working relationship with the large tourism industry in their country. Among its many activities it conducts training seminars for German tour guides who are leading tour groups to developing countries. Tourism Watch also presents annual awards to media groups (the Toura d'Or award) plus another set of awards to tourism projects in developing countries which meet the criteria of social responsibility (TO DO awards). These presentations always get wide publicity within the trade in Germany and beyond.

One effective action of Tourism Watch has been to publish *Sympathy*, a colourful little magazine which deals honestly with tourism questions. It is published from time to time on a specific theme such as a particular region of the world or a related issue. A series on world religions was greeted as especially helpful. The books are purchased in large numbers by travel agents who distribute them as a supplement to their usual guide books. In 25 years, 47 different titles have been produced with a total circulation of approximately 5 million copies.

Few other countries have given much attention to the tourists leaving their shores, although church programmes have been initiated in countries such as the United States, United Kingdom and Australia, mostly as part of their overseas aid programmes.

In European tourist-receiving countries the church has been forced to look more seriously at tourism since their buildings have become popular tourist stops. Indeed the great cathedrals of Europe are now so well patronized by tour groups that many of them now charge a substantial admission fee and, in some cases, have to restrict the number of people entering the building.

This raises a different set of problems for the church. If the cathedral is so crowded with chattering tourists, where do people find space to pray? And when the cathedral is crowded by tourists and almost empty for worship, what witness is the church giving? When tourism began to boom in the 1970s English cathedrals started to realize that the crowds of tourists entering their building represented both an opportunity to witness and a threat to their existence. With the help of the World Council of Churches, a unique conference was held in 1975 at Windsor Castle, the home of Queen Elizabeth II, which also houses the historic St George's Chapel. Even in those early years of tourism the chapel was in danger of being over-run by tourists. The conference brought together a number of well-known musicians, dancers and artists plus theologians and church leaders. The intention was to spend ten days together exploring ways to make this Christian centre speak to the thousands of tourists who passed through it and to help them understand something significant about the Christian religion.

With the approval of the castle authorities, the group at Windsor experimented over several days with creative plays, music, displays, lighting, prayer rooms, songs, moments of silence and docents in an attempt to find ways to give the cathedral more Christian relevance to visitors. Through interviews and questions they assessed the response of tourists and not surprisingly it was very mixed. A few of the changes were appreciated but mostly the tourists responded with puzzlement. They did not seem to be interested in being educated about the religious meaning of the church and a few made it quite clear they didn't come to this place to have to listen to any "religious stuff". The conference participants could not come up with clear solutions. Nor have any subsequent gatherings been able to decide what is the best way to run a tourist-focused cathedral. Some have, in fact, concluded that when cathedrals become major tourist attractions they no longer have contemporary Christian relevance and should be recognized as simply a museum to past history, to be administered by a national historical trust.

Outside Europe, in what was once called the third world, the churches had a problem of a different kind. Christians in developing countries were seeing their culture, their customs and their environment under threat and were seeking ways to counter this situation. The island of Bali in Indonesia was the first of the developing countries in Asia to play host to mass tourism and the church took a unique stance. From the beginning of the tourism rush in the late 1960s, the church in Bali regarded the invasion of the foreigners as a very significant part of their ministry. They soon recognized that there was injustice in the way tourism was operating. A village group of around 40 people would be asked to perform one of their exciting monkey dances (in abbreviated form) for the tourists. On researching the issue, church leaders found that each of the 100 or so tourists paid the organizer US$6 each to watch the performance but when the performance was finished the village would be paid the Balinese equivalent of $20 in total.

The church undertook to stop the exploitation of its members and sought ways to use tourism for the benefit of Balinese people. Church people themselves were first conscientized to understand what was happening and then they were assisted to develop their skills. The church organized the first tourism training school on the island and in 1977 completed the building of a meditation centre, called Dhyana Pura, at which conferences could be held and where young Balinese could learn tourism vocational skills.

The Balinese church has proved itself to be extremely flexible. It is one of the few churches that came into existence without any foreign missionary influence in either its establishment or early years and so was able to develop a largely indigenous form of architecture, worship and structure. Without foreign funding, Balinese clergy became "worker priests" and most became directly involved in tourism developments.

Unfortunately, examples such as Germany and Bali are rather rare in church circles. Relatively few people in the churches have seen tourism as an issue of any significance and it barely rates a mention in church conferences or statements. Local churches in the third world might sometimes get anxious about injustice and bishops might wonder what they can do with their cathedrals but the larger picture of tourism has usually been ignored by church leaders.

There has been one interesting exception to this generalization. The late Pope John Paul II has been, in recent years, an articulate and informed spokesperson on issues relating to tourism. An ardent traveller himself, he has been sending out strong annual messages to the tourism industry and to tourists themselves. These became more emphatic in relation to the world's inequalities. In 2003 he reaffirmed "a principle which is self-evident yet often ignored: our goal should not be the benefit of a privileged few, but rather the improvement of the living conditions of all". Applying this to tourism, he spoke of tourists visiting countries where there is poverty and hunger and in such cases, he said "(the tourists) should resist the temptation to retreat into a sort of 'happy cocoon' distancing themselves from the social context, rather they should refrain from profiting from their own privileged position to exploit the needs of the locals". He urged tourists to enter into genuine dialogue "among persons of equal dignity" so that there will be sincere openness expressed in "concrete gestures of solidarity". [31]

The pope was unusually frank in his challenge to tourism. In his message in 2002 he spoke of the ecological emergency being faced by the planet and condemned "a certain kind of savage tourism (which) has contributed to and still contributes to this unwanted destruction by way of tourist installations built without any planning that respects their impact on the environment".[32]

The pope's challenge should resonate with all Christians. At its heart, the gospel is a call to love God through loving our neighbour. When our neighbours are hungry, we are required to feed them and when they suffer Christ also suffers. This basic fact of Christian life underlies all that we have been saying about tourism. In travel we meet our neighbours face to face and we must have a degree of concern for their situation. When this travel takes place in developing countries we must know whether our presence improves the life of the people or adds yet another burden to an already inhuman situation. Travel does not take place in a vacuum, other people are implicated in and by our actions. There are economic and cultural implications which have to be assessed.

Like life itself, travel takes the Christian on a journey, both outward and inward. It is part of a life-long quest for meaning and wholeness. If we travel with cultural sensitivity and an open mind to issues of injustice there are life-changing experiences waiting as we meet people with a cultural background and view of life that may be completely different from our own. Travel is a privilege which we need to respect.

9. Towards the Future

A code of ethics for tourism

With such diverse and complex problems, we are faced with a persistent question: How can the tourism industry be regulated? Governments are the obvious first choice for this monitoring but when tourism comes to a small developing country, governments often lack the will or even the power to control the activities of tourism developers or of the tourists themselves. Taken as a whole, the tourism industry now has incredible power over smaller countries. A reduction in the tourist flow can cripple a country's economic situation, while the introduction of new airlines or new hotel resorts can bring a helpful injection of new money. Unfortunately for developing countries, these decisions are usually taken at business meetings in affluent countries and reinforce the powerless situation of a country dependent on the goodwill of foreign interests.

In recent years, the World Tourism Organization (WTO) has moved slowly towards the development of a more regulatory framework for tourism that can protect all the stake-holders from the worst aspects of tourism. In October 1999, after years of deliberation, the WTO general assembly approved the Global Code of Ethics for Tourism.[33] The code is a huge step forward for the industry and indicates that at least some of its members are aware of the negative aspects of tourism. The code includes nine articles outlining the "rules of the game" for destinations, governments, tour operators, developers, travel agents, workers and travellers themselves.

The really distinctive feature of the code is in the final article which makes provision for the redress of grievances. It is unique for such industry codes to include a mechanism for enforcement and time will indicate how effective this will be. A committee of experts has already been formed and will meet regularly to promote the code and to act as a conciliatory body in cases of disputes between tourism stake-holders.

According to Francesco Frangialli, the secretary general of WTO, the aim is to "develop tourism on the basis of sound and fundamental values. Tourism development should be an activity that serves humanity and provides more than only material benefits to people."[34]

Important as this document is, there are contradictions that cannot be resolved by stating them in a code.

The tourism industry places emphasis on article 13 of the Universal Declaration of Human Rights which guarantees the right of liberty of movement from one country to another and this right is reiterated in the code of ethics. But the Declaration of Human Rights also contains article 22 which affirms that each person is entitled to "realization of the economic, social and cultural rights indispensable for his dignity and the free development of his personality". There is an inevitable clash between the rights to freedom of movement and the rights to live unaffected by the cultural and ecological impacts of tourism. Indigenous peoples have been among the first to raise this difficulty with the code. At what point does freedom of movement cease? The code speaks of facilitating "the maximum freedom of travel" but when this intrudes on a people's culture it is in conflict with other rights. And how far can freedom of movement be allowed in the fragile environments of the planet?

Some tourism activists have dismissed the code as "shoring up the ailing tourism industry". They argue that the code is too sympathetic to the market economy and will reinforce all the inequities apparent in globalization.[35]

All intergovernmental documents end up being a compromise and the code of ethics is no exception. Some parts of the tourism industry believe it goes too far in recognizing tourism's involvement in the negative impact of tourism, while NGOs argue it does not go far enough. In the midst of this balancing act it is to be hoped that the code of ethics will enable changes to be implemented. So far it has had almost universal political support from the United Nations and individual governments. The test of the code's effectiveness will come when it has to rule on some of the crises which continue to be inherent in tourism development.

Other organizations have also been developing codes of conduct based on specific aspects of tourism. A significant example of cooperation was initiated by European ECPAT groups with the support of international tourism agencies. They drew up a code of conduct to protect children from sexual exploitation in travel and tourism which is based on a cooperative agreement between national groups of tourism companies and ECPAT. The partners who have signed the code include some of the largest tour operators in Europe. They have agreed to share information and work cooperatively with ECPAT in projects and training sessions designed to protect children (for details see appendix).

The programme has worked successfully in Sweden, Germany, Netherlands, Italy, Austria and the United Kingdom for years. Recently the code of conduct has been adopted by the North American tourism industry where it is supported by both ECPAT and UNICEF.

A code of conduct for tourists

Having himself witnessed at first hand the torments and debasement of human nature, the traveller should make

> known the misfortune of others to those who have the power to help.
>
> Alexander von Humboldt, 1769-1859

Tourism has curious twists. Instead of the product being sent, sold or given to the consumer as usually happens in trade deals, the consumer goes to the tourism product directly. In ordinary transactions, the character of the consumer is irrelevant to the product but in tourism the character and conduct of the consumer play a significant role in the success of the "transaction".

So what are we to make of tourist behaviour? As we have seen, there are ugly tourists and good tourists. There are situations where tourists are attacked by angry locals and places where they are welcomed as brothers and sisters. How should a person act in order to be a responsible tourist?

There have been many attempts to write a code of conduct for tourists. One of the first to be recorded was written at a small consultation organized by the Christian Conference of Asia in Penang 1975. It was soon picked up by the secular press and with small amendments has been reproduced thousands of times ever since. Thirty years on and large tourism companies such as *Fodors* are still reproducing it in some of their publications.

Here is the original text:

1. Travel in a spirit of humility and with a genuine desire to learn more about the people of your host country.
2. Be sensitively aware of the feelings of other people, thus preventing what might be offensive behaviour on your part.
3. Cultivate the habit of listening and observing rather than merely hearing and seeing.

4. Realize that often the people in the country you visit have time, concepts and thought patterns different from your own; this does not make them inferior, only different.
5. Instead of looking for that "beach paradise" discover the enrichment of seeing a different way of life through other eyes.
6. Acquaint yourself with local customs – people will be happy to help you.
7. Instead of the Western practice of "knowing all the answers" cultivate the habit of asking questions.
8. Remember you are only one of thousands of tourists visiting this country and do not expect special privileges.
9. If you really want your experience to be a "home away from home" it is foolish to waste money on travelling.
10. When you are shopping remember that "bargain" you obtained was only possible because of the low wages paid to the maker.
11. Do not make promises to people in your host country unless you are certain you can carry them through.
12. Spend time reflecting on your daily experiences in an attempt to deepen your understanding. It is said that "what enriches you may rob and violate others".

It is a slightly idealistic image of tourism but is written in simple language that continues to make it relevant to tourists. Since being written, dozens of other organizations have drafted a code of conduct aimed at persuading tourists to travel responsibly.

Tourism continues to throw up new situations and these need to be kept in mind when considering the actions of tourists. Any contemporary code of conduct will have to include such things as the threats to the environment, the problems of human rights and the sexual exploitation of children by child sex tourists.

In 2005, the World Tourism Organization built on its code of ethics by drafting a code of conduct for tourists called "The Responsible Tourist and Traveller". The code begins with a statement extracted from the global code of ethics:

> Travel and tourism should be planned and practised as a privileged means of individual and collective fulfillment; when practised with a sufficiently open mind, it is an irreplaceable factor of self-education, mutual tolerance and learning about the legitimate differences between peoples and cultures and their diversity. Everyone has a role to play creating responsible travel and tourism. Governments, business and communities must do all they can, but as a guest you can support this in many ways.

And while the sentiments are genuine and true, one cannot imagine any tourists pinning it to the wall to remind them that their trip is being "planned as a privileged means of individual and collective fulfillment…."

No. I believe we are past the stage where we must have long lists of rules or explanations. If it is our purpose to influence the behaviour of tourists we need something more like a tourist promise based on simple principles such as the following:

As a tourist:

I will respect the customs and life-style of the people I meet.

I will do nothing to harm the environment.

I will at all times try to avoid exploiting local people.

In the end, that is really what we want from all travellers. Tourists have to work out for themselves how they respond to each situation they face and we cannot anticipate what these situations will be. But if we travel with an attitude of respect for people and the environment plus recognition of the economic and social rights of those visited, we have covered most of the critical situations which will arise. That is what it means to be a responsible tourist.

10. Bon Voyage

We have condensed far too much information into this book but that is the reality of tourism. The size and complexity of the tourism movement is quite daunting, even for those who study its activity full-time. But whatever the situation today, we know that things are not going to get any easier in the coming years. Workers in most tourist-sending countries are getting longer holiday time, the cost of travel continues to go down and the amount of disposable income is increasing. The inevitable conclusion from these facts is that, despite the threat of oil shortages, tourism will continue to grow at a dramatic rate in the foreseeable future.

It is salutary to sit in the comfort of our home and realize that in the next 24 hours at least another 3 million tourists will be leaving their homes to travel to a foreign tourist destination and to know that another 3 million will travel tomorrow and tomorrow and every day this year. It is even more incredible to read the predictions and discover that in less than 15 years from now there will probably be 4,500,000 international tourists leaving home every day.

This vision of the future sounds a little like the biblical image of the plague of locusts. The writer of Exodus speaks of the locusts, "There will be so many that they will completely cover the ground. They will eat everything. They will fill your palaces and the houses of all your officials and all your people. They will be worse than your ancestors ever saw."[36]

Of course the analogy should not be taken too far and the indiscriminate destruction wrought by a plague of locusts is more visibly extreme and immediate than any damage caused by tourists. Even so, there is the degradation of the environment and destruction of culture caused by uncontrolled mass tourism that can in some circumstance be as destructive a force as any locust plague.

The incredible growth of tourism over the past 55 years has changed society and life-styles and contributed to the creation of a more open, globalized world. It has also contributed to a more divided world, bringing disaster to communities and individuals. Our inability to find a satisfactory balance between the positive and negative affects of tourism is a continuing challenge to governments and the wider society. Meanwhile the full significance of this great wave of travelling human beings is passing us by and reflects the fact that we are dealing with a completely new social phenomenon in world history. It poses a threat we do not yet fully understand.

We cannot be sure where tourism will lead us in the coming decades. It may develop into new and creative directions that will benefit humankind or it may usher in an era of human and environmental degradation. What is clear is that we must all begin to take this extraordinary social phenomena more seriously and work to ensure that it becomes a force for peace and justice. What happens tomorrow in tourism is dependent on today's decisions. The future is in our hands.

And now it only remains for me to bid you au revoir and wish you "bon voyage".

My guess is that 90 percent of those of you reading this book will be planning to travel somewhere internationally in the next months. If your travel is for a holiday, then you have already been bombarded with ideas about *where* to travel. But this book asks you to examine the more direct questions: *How* will you travel and *why*? Our best hope is that you will travel with a receptive mind: Listening to the voices of those you meet and reflecting on your actions. Try to look behind the scenes and learn what tourism is doing to the people – especially if you travel in a developing country. As Pope John Paul II reminded us, don't travel in "a happy cocoon".

Above all else I wish you a journey that will challenge your thinking:

May you meet interesting people
May you be overwhelmed by the beauty and diversity of our world
May your journey contribute to the enrichment of your hosts
And may you return home a better person.

11. Appendix

Some tourism links

There are numerous organizations dealing with local or specific aspects of tourism and these can be found listed in most tourism web-sites. Below is a short list of some of the organizations referred to in this book for those wishing to obtain further information on any of the issues raised.

The Ecumenical Coalition on Tourism (ECOT - formerly ECTWT) 96 Pak Tin Village Area 2, Mei Tin Road, Shatin, NT, Hong Kong, www.ecotonline.org

A coalition of church and secular agencies established in 1982 working to negate the undesirable aspects of modern tourism and in its place institute socially responsible and ethically oriented tourism. ECOT believes that tourism must be based on justice and sustainability for host communities and that therefore tourism planning and practice must be democratized.

ECPAT International (End Child Prostitution, Child Pornography and Trafficking in Children for Sexual Purposes) 328 Phyathai Road, Bangkok 10400, Thailand, www.ecpat.net

Begun in 1991 as a result of ECOT action and now an independent coalition with 73 groups in 67 countries, ECOT "seeks to encourage the world community to ensure that children everywhere enjoy their fundamental rights free from all forms of commercial sexual exploitation".

Tourism Concern Stapleton House, 277-281 Holloway Road, London N7 8HN, Great Britain, www.tourismconcern.org.uk

An organization campaigning for ethical and fairly traded tourism.

Tourism Watch Ulrich-von-Hassell-Straße 76, D-53123 Bonn, Germany, www.tourism-watch.de

The agency of the German churches which works with tourism agencies and German tourists and convenes an association of European church agencies dealing with tourism.

United Nations Environmental Programme (UNEP) 39-43, Quai André Citroën, 75739 Paris, Cedex 15, France, www.uneptie.org/tourism

UNEP is the main UN focal point for the promotion of sustainable tourism among government agencies and the industry.

World Tourism Organization (WTO/OMT) Capitán Haya 42,28020 Madrid, Spain, www.world-tourism.org

The leading international organization in tourism now has a membership of 145 countries, seven territories and over 300 affiliate members from the private sector.

Abbreviations

ECOT	Ecumenical Coalition on Tourism
ECPAT	End Child Prostitution, Child Pornography and Trafficking in Children for Sexual Purposes
ECTWT	Ecumenical Coalition on Third World Tourism (now ECOT)
IAATO	International Association of Antarctic Tour Operators
IYE	International Year of Ecotourism (UN)
NGO	non-governmental organization
UN	United Nations

UNCTAD	United Nations Committee on Trade and Development
UNEP	United Nations Environmental Programme
UNESCO	United Nations Educational, Social and Cultural Organization.
UNICEF	United Nations Children's Fund
WCC	World Council of Churches
WTO	World Tourism Organization

The code of conduct

The international development of the code is promoted by an international, multi-stakeholder steering committee composed of prestigious tourism industry representatives, non-governmental organizations and UN agencies. The secretariat is based in ECPAT New York.

Suppliers of tourism services adopting the code commit themselves to implement the following six criteria:

1. To establish an ethical policy regarding commercial sexual exploitation of children.
2. To train the personnel in the country of origin and travel destinations.
3. To introduce a clause in contracts with suppliers, stating a common repudiation of commercial sexual exploitation of children.
4. To provide information to travellers by means of catalogues, brochures, in-flight films, ticket-slips, home pages, etc.
5. To provide information to local "key persons" at the destinations.
6. To report annually

For more information see www.thecode.org

Notes

[1] Mayer Hillman, Town & Country Planning Magazine, September 1996.

[2] The Berlin Declaration on Sustainable Tourism, 1997 Point 16. United Nations Environmental Programme (UNEP)

[3] WTO-UNEP Concept Paper - International Year of Ecotourism 2002

[4] WTO-UNEP Concept Paper - International Year of Ecotourism 2002 Objectives (d)

[5] The UN Commission on Sustainable Development, New York. Seventh Session, 19-30 April 1999, Tourism and Sustainable Development - Non-Government Organization Statement.

[6] UN Conference on Climate Change, Buenos Aires, 2004

[7] *Wilderness and Environmental Medicine*, June 2005, reporting on a survey of 132 climbers

[8] *Newsweek*, August 1992. Quoted in *Contours* magazine, September 1992

[9] http://www.mountainpartnership.org/themes/i-tourism.html

[10] *The Economist*, 9 April 2005. P.28,29.

[11] *Contours* magazine October-December 1999

[12] Source: *Our Planet*, UNEP magazine for environmentally sustainable development, volume 10, no. 3, 1999

[13] These agreements include: Biological Diversity, Climate Change, Regional Seas, Marine Impacts from Land-Based Activities, Migratory Species, CITES, Ramsar, World Heritage.

[14] *Cannibal Tours,* a film by Peter O'Rourke, 1988. Distribution Direct Cinema Ltd

[15] Researchers from the Centre for Public Health at Liverpool John Moores University surveyed young holidaymakers in 2000, 2001 and 2002.

[16] The Conference was organized by the Ecumenical Coalition on Third World Tourism, (now named the Ecumenical Coalition on Tourism) and followed research in Thailand, Taiwan, Sri Lanka and the Philippines. It gave rise to the organization ECPAT International.

[17] UNICEF, State of the World's Children, 2005

[18] The World Tourism Organization, Global Code of Ethics for Tourism, Adopted September 1999

[19] Travel Trade Gazette, 9 February 1973

[20] Interview with journalist Ron Gluckman www.gluckman.com

[21] The Nation, quoted in *Contours*, July-September 2001

[22] http://www.uneptie.org/pc/tourism/sust-tourism/economic.htm

[23] UNCTAD figures quoted by UNEP
http://www.uneptie.org/pc/tourism/sust-tourism/economic.htm

[24] Stecker, B. (1996): Ecotourism: Potential for Conservation and Sustainable Use of Tropical Forests. A case study on the national parks Taman Negara and Endau-Rompin in Malaysia.

[25] NGO report to Commission on Sustainable Development, Seventh Session19-30 April 1999, New York

[26] Quoted in *Tourism in Focus*, magazine of Tourism Concern, summer 2004 p.9. Tourism Concern has launched a programme to combat poverty in the Maldives

[27] Dr Jose Luis Rubio, European Society for Soil and Water Conservation – http://www.responsibletravel.com/Copy/Copy101765.htm

[28] *ibid* Source *The Independent*

[29] www.atan.org/en/

[30] Third World Tourism Workshop Report, ed. Ron O'Grady, Sept 1980. CCA

[31] Message of John Paul II for the 24th World Day of Tourism, 27 Sept 2003

[32] Message of John Paul II for the 23rd World Day of Tourism, 27 Sept 2002

[33] Global Code of Ethics for Tourism go to www.world-tourism.org.

[34] Francesco Frangialli, dialogue on tourism, cultural diversity and sustainable development, Barcelona, 14-16 July 2004

[35] T.T. Srikumaar "Why Do We Need an Alternative Code of Ethics for Tourism?" in *Contours* January-April 2003

[36] Book of Exodus, Chapter 10.